# Microsoft® Windows® XP Home Edition

**MINUTE GUIDE**

201 West 103rd Street
Indianapolis, IN 46290

**Shelley O'Hara**

**Ten Minute Guide to Microsoft® Windows® XP, Home Edition**



International Standard Book Number: 0-7897-2737-4

Library of Congress Catalog Card Number: 2001098162

Printed in the United States of America

First Printing: February 2002

05 04 03 7 6 5

## Trademarks

All terms mentioned in this book that are known to be trademarks or service marks have been appropriately capitalized. Que cannot attest to the accuracy of this information. Use of a term in this book should not be regarded as affecting the validity of any trademark or service mark.

## Warning and Disclaimer

Every effort has been made to make this book as complete and as accurate as possible, but no warranty or fitness is implied. The information provided is on an "as is" basis. The author and the publisher shall have neither liability nor responsibility to any person or entity with respect to any loss or damages arising from the information contained in this book.

**Associate Publisher**
Greg Wiegand

**Acquisitions Editor**
Stephanie J. McComb

**Development Editor**
Todd Brakke

**Managing Editor**
Thomas F. Hayes

**Project Editor**
Karen S. Shields

**Production Editor**
Candice Hightower

**Indexer**
Mandie Frank

**Proofreaders**
Maribeth Echard
Harvey Stanbrough

**Team Coordinator**
Sharry Lee Gregory

**Interior Designer**
Gary Adair

**Cover Designer**
Alan Clements

**Page Layout**
Susan Geiselman

# Contents

## Dedication

*To my nieces, Alana and Stephanie, who bring so much pride and joy into my life.*

## Acknowledgments

Thanks to Stephanie McComb for inviting me to do this project. Also, I appreciate the suggestions, editing, and fine-tuning of Todd Brakke, Kyle Bryant, Karen Shields, and Candice Hightower.

## Tell Us What You Think!

As the reader of this book, *you* are our most important critic and commentator. We value your opinion and want to know what we're doing right, what we could do better, what areas you'd like to see us publish in, and any other words of wisdom you're willing to pass our way.

As an associate publisher for Que, I welcome your comments. You can fax, e-mail, or write me directly to let me know what you did or didn't like about this book—as well as what we can do to make our books stronger.

*Please note that I cannot help you with technical problems related to the topic of this book, and that due to the high volume of mail I receive, I might not be able to reply to every message.*

When you write, please be sure to include this book's title and author as well as your name and phone or fax number. I will carefully review your comments and share them with the author and editors who worked on the book.


Fax: 317-581-4666

E-mail: `feedback@quepublishing.com`

Mail: Greg Wiegand<br>
Que<br>
201 West 103rd Street<br>
Indianapolis, IN 46290 USA

# Introduction

Microsoft Windows XP is the newest version of the Windows operating system, first made available in the fall of 2001. This new version gives a total makeover of existing Windows versions, making features easier to use and providing new versions of programs, such as Windows Movie Maker and Internet Explorer. Lesson 1, "What's New in Windows XP," gives a more detailed summary of the new version of Windows XP.

## New Users and Upgraders

If you recently purchased a computer, it probably came with Windows XP installed. If so, this is the perfect book for getting you started using Windows XP. You learn the basics of performing all the key tasks for using a computer including starting programs, saving your work, sending e-mail, browsing the Internet, and more.

If you have upgraded or are thinking of upgrading, this book can help you get up to speed on the new look of Windows as well as help you learn about the new features. Should you upgrade? Probably so. The new version not only includes a revamped interface, but also has behind-the-scenes changes that make this version more stable (less prone to crashing) and more intuitive.

## Conventions Used in This Book

You can use this guide in any number of ways. You can read it from start to finish. The topics are arranged from the most basic to the more advanced. Or you can use the table of contents to find a topic of interest, and then read that lesson. You can find lessons on all major aspects of using Windows XP. If you are looking for a particular topic, you can also use the index to find the exact pages where the topic is covered.

The book includes many step-by-step explanations of how to perform common tasks. You can easily follow along. Figures also illustrate key points so that you have a visual guide to the instructions as well.

To help you move through the lessons easily, these conventions are used:

| | |
|---|---|
| Onscreen text | Onscreen text appears in **bold** type. |
| Text you should type | Information you need to type appears in a **`monospace bold`** type. |
| Items you select | Commands, options, and icons you are to select and keys you are to press appear in **bold** type. |

In telling you to choose menu commands, this book uses the format *menu title, menu command.* For example, the statement "choose **File, Properties**" means to "open the File menu and select the Properties command."

In addition to those conventions, the *10 Minute Guide* uses the following icons to identify helpful information:

**PLAIN ENGLISH**

New or unfamiliar terms are defined in term sidebars.

**TIP**

Read these tips for ideas that cut corners and confusion.

**CAUTION**

This identifies areas where new users often run into trouble; these tips offer practical solutions to those problems.

# LESSON 1
# What's New in Windows XP

*In this lesson you learn about the new and updated features of Microsoft Windows XP.*

## CHECKING OUT THE REVAMPED START MENU

Windows XP, introduced in fall 2001, is the newest version of Windows. The biggest visible change to this version is the updated Start button and menu. Click the Start button to display the menu (see Figure 1.1). Notice the left side lists commonly used programs, while the right half provides access to Windows XP commands.

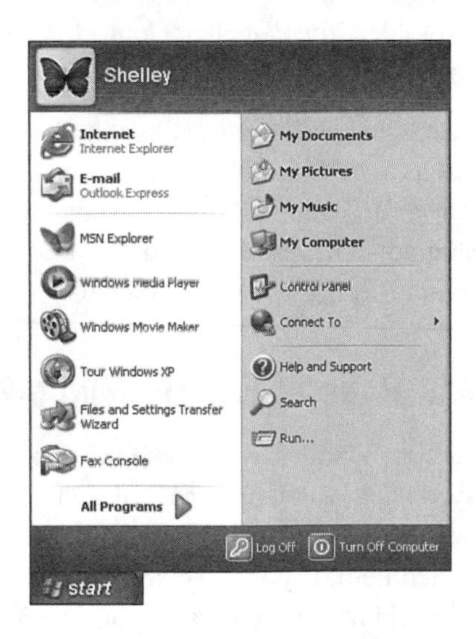


**FIGURE 1.1**
*Note the new look of the desktop, including the Start button and menu.*

At the top-left corner of the Start menu, Windows XP always lists the programs for accessing the Internet and e-mail (by default Internet Explorer and Outlook Express, both programs included with Windows XP). Beneath that you see your six most often used programs. As a shortcut, you can click any of these programs to start the program.

**Change the Start Menu** You can change the menu, adding other programs to the left pane, for example. See Lesson 16, "Setting Up Programs," later in this book.

If the program you want to launch is not listed, you can use the new All Programs menu to display a list of all the program folders and programs. This menu is similar to the classic Windows Start menu.

If you look at the right pane, you see Windows XP folders and commands. For example, you can use My Documents to display the contents of this system folder. You can click Control Panel to open Windows XP's Control Panel.

At the bottom of the Start menu, you can use the Log Off button to log off. This feature is used for multiple users. See Lesson 18, "Setting Up Windows for Multiple Users or Networking," for more information. To shut down or restart, use the Turn Off Computer button, covered in Lesson 17, "Maintaining Your PC."

## USING THE TASK PANE IN FOLDER WINDOWS

Another new feature of Windows XP is how the contents of drives and folders are displayed when using programs like My Computer or File Explorer. The new view includes a task pane that lists common commands for the selected item. If you select a folder, for example, you see commands for working with folders. If you select a file, you see commands for working with files. If you select a picture, you see commands for working with pictures (see Figure 1.2).

**FIGURE 1.2**
*Rather than remember which menu or button to use, you can use the more descriptive task pane commands to work with folders and files.*

**TIP**

**Change the View** Windows XP also enables you to change how the contents of a folder window are displayed. See Lesson 6, "Managing Files," and Lesson 7, "Finding Files," for more information.

The inclusion of the My Documents icon in the Start menu is another change. Notice that the Windows desktop does not include the My Documents and My Computer folder by default. You access these and other common folders, such as My Pictures, from the Start menu. Click the Start button, and then click the folder name. If you prefer, you can add icons for these folders to the desktop as covered in Lesson 2, "Understanding the Windows XP Desktop."

## USING THE CONTROL PANEL

To make most customization changes, use the Control Panel. You can use the icons in this system feature to customize the display, change the mouse, add a new printer, and make other common changes. In previous versions, all icons were listed in one window. In Windows XP, the Control Panel icons are grouped by category (see Figure 1.3). You can more easily find and understand which options are available in this view.

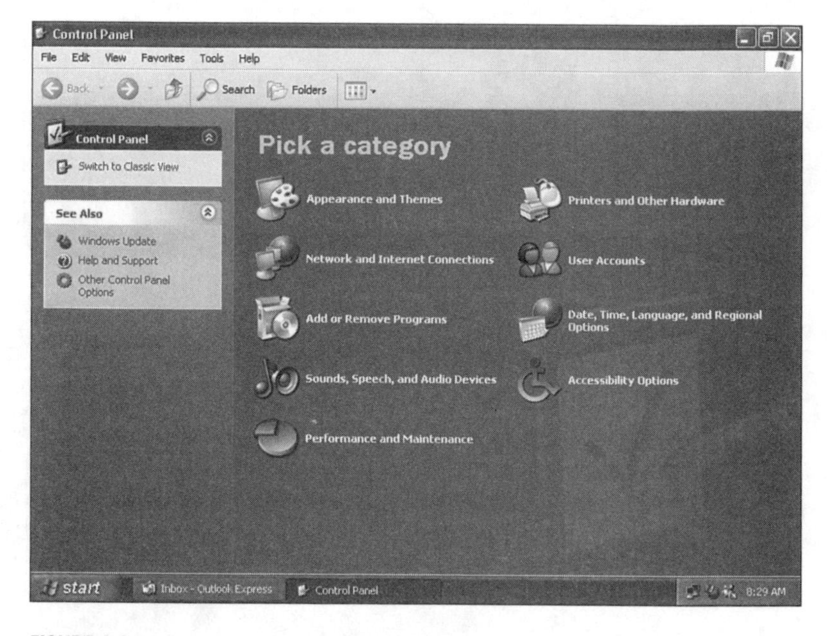


**FIGURE 1.3**
*To display the Control Panel choose **Start, Control Panel**. You can click any of the categories to display the features in that category.*

TIP

**Use Classic View** If you prefer to use the original view or if you can't find the Control Panel icon you need, switch to Classic View by clicking the Switch to Classic View command in the task pane.

## Learning About Other Windows XP Highlights

In addition to these major changes, note some new additions and changes to other features. The following is a brief highlight of each feature as well as a reference for finding more information:

- **Internet Explorer 6**—Windows XP includes a new version of Internet Explorer. This version includes new security features as well as some subtle changes to the look of the browser window. Lesson 10, "Browsing the Internet," covers this program.
- **Windows Messenger**—You can use Windows Messenger to send and receive instant messages. See Lesson 9, "Sending E-mail," for more information.
- **User Accounts**—If more than one person uses your computer, you can set up user accounts so that each person can customize Windows XP to suit his fancy. Lesson 18 covers this topic.

In this lesson you learned about the new look and features of Windows XP. Lesson 2 discusses the Windows XP desktop—the jumping-off point for all tasks.

# LESSON 2
# Understanding the Windows XP Desktop

*In this lesson you learn about the Microsoft Windows XP desktop. After your PC boots and you successfully log on, this is what you see.*

## WHAT'S ON THE DESKTOP?

The desktop, your starting place, provides access to all the programs and files on your computer (see Figure 2.1).

Here's a quick overview of what you see:

- The desktop is the background area. You can place icons on the desktop for fast access to programs and folders.
- The Start button is used to display the Start menu (covered in the next section).
- The taskbar displays a button for any windows or programs that are open. In Figure 2.1, Outlook Express is open. You can click the taskbar button to display this program window.
- The system tray includes status icons for current tasks. For example, if you are printing, you see a printer icon. If you are connected to the Internet, you see a connection icon. For more on the system tray, see the section "Viewing the Task Bar and System Tray" later in this lesson.
- Desktop icons provide access to commonly used programs, folders, and files. The only icon that appears by default is the Recycle Bin. You can add other icons. See the section "Working with Desktop Icons" later in this lesson.

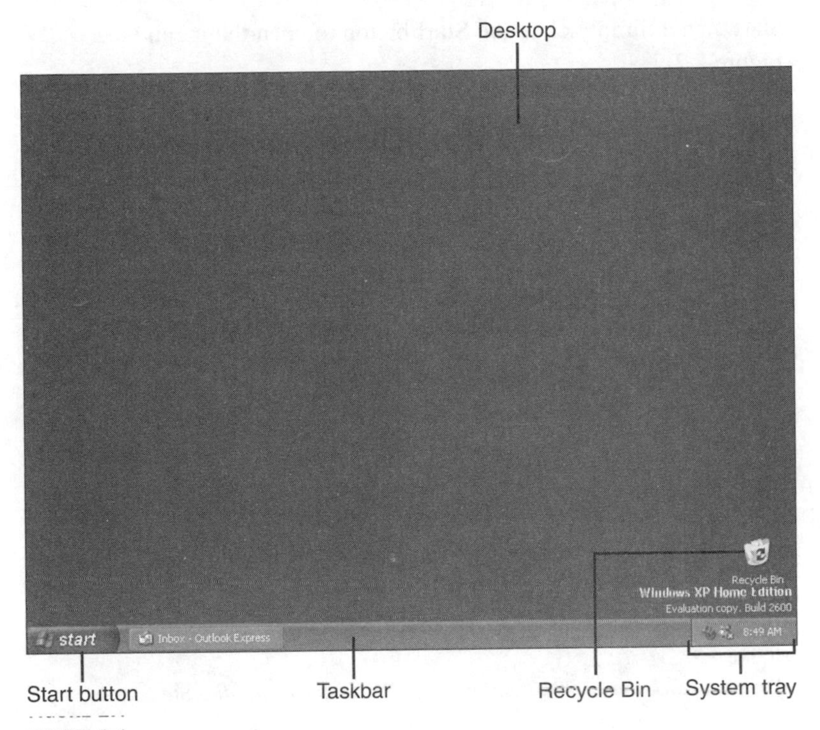


**FIGURE 2.1**
*The new desktop is pretty bare and uncluttered.*

**TIP**

**Change the Desktop Background** You can change the appearance of the desktop. See Lesson 15, "Customizing the Windows XP Desktop," for more information.

## Displaying the Start Menu

When you want to open a folder or start a program use the Start menu. As discussed in Lesson 1, "What's New in Windows XP," the Start menu in Windows XP has a new look, so if you are upgrading from a previous version, take a look at how the Start menu is organized. If you are new to Windows XP, you'll find it's easy to use the

Start menu. Simply click the Start button to open the menu (see Figure 2.2).

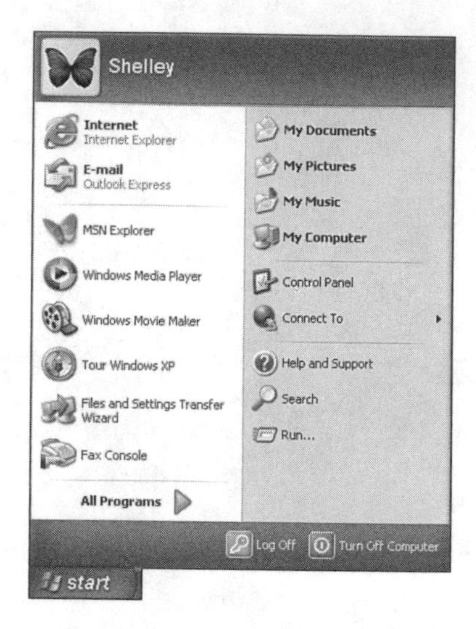


**FIGURE 2.2**
*When you click the Start button, you see the commands in the Start menu.*

At the top of the menu, you see the programs you use for the Internet and e-mail. You can click the appropriate command to start the program. For instance, to start your e-mail program, click **E-mail**.

Beneath the Internet and e-mail programs, you see the six most often used programs. This list makes it easy to start frequently used programs. Click the program name to start that program. What you see in your Start menu is different from what appears in Figure 2.2. You see the programs you use most often and your selected Internet and e-mail programs.

If the program you want to start is not listed, you can click All Programs to list all the program folders and programs on your computer. You learn more about starting programs in Lesson 3, "Starting Programs."

Rather than include desktop icons for folders (as in previous versions), Windows XP lists the folders on the Start menu. You can click any of these folders—My Documents, My Pictures, My Music, or My Computer—to open that folder. See Lesson 5, "Using My Computer to Organize Your Folders," for more information on opening folders.

In addition to folders, Windows XP lists commands such as Control Panel, Connect To, Help and Support, Search, and Run. Click the command you want to execute.

When you are done working with Windows, you can turn off your computer using the Turn Off Computer button. If someone else uses the computer, you can log off or switch users using the Log Off button so that this person can log on.

TIP

**Restart the Computer** If your computer gets stuck or if you make changes to key system features, you may need to restart. Click Turn Off Computer, and then select Restart. For more information on shutting down the computer and restarting, see Lesson 17, "Maintaining Your PC."

## Working with Desktop Icons

By default, the Windows XP displays the Recycle Bin on the desktop. You can add other shortcut icons so that you have convenient access to your most often used programs, folders, and files. A common addition is placing icons for My Computer and My Documents on the desktop.

To add My Documents, My Computer, or My Network Places icons to the desktop, follow these steps:

1. Right-click a blank area of the desktop to display the shortcut menu.
2. Click the **Properties** command. You see the Display Properties dialog box.

3. Click the **Desktop** tab to display these options.
4. Click the **Customize Desktop** button.
5. On the General tab, shown in Figure 2.3, check any of the icons you want displayed. For instance, to add the My Documents folder to the desktop, click the **My Documents** check box.
6. When you are done, click **OK**. Any icon you checked now appears on the desktop.

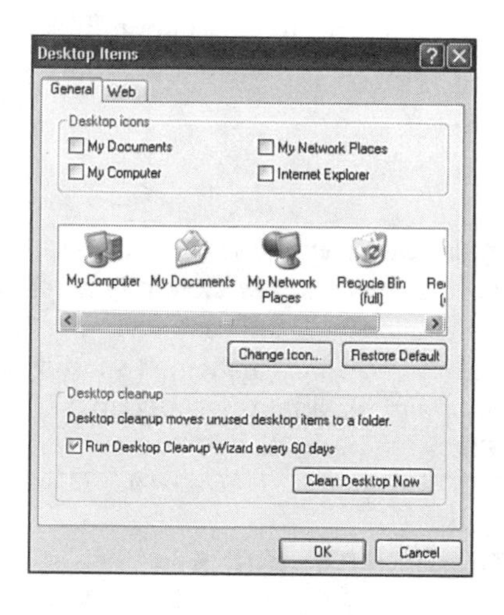


**FIGURE 2.3**
*Use this dialog box to add desktop icons to the desktop and to change the appearance of these icons.*

**TIP**

**Create Folder and File Shortcuts** To create shortcut icons to other folders or files, display that folder or file. Right-click the folder or file, and then select **Send To**, **Desktop** (create shortcut).

In addition to folder shortcuts, you can add icons for programs. To add a program shortcut to the desktop, see Lesson 16, "Setting Up Programs."

After you've added icons, you can move, delete, and rename icons on the desktop as needed:

- To move an icon, click it while holding down the mouse button, and then drag it to the location you want.
- To delete an icon, click it, and then press the **Delete** key. Confirm the deletion by clicking **Yes**. Note that if you delete a program shortcut icon you are not deleting the program, just the icon. To remove the program, uninstall it as covered in Lesson 16, "Setting Up Programs."
- To change the name of an icon, right-click the icon and then select **Rename**. Type a new name and press **Enter**.

## Viewing the Taskbar and System Tray

The taskbar, as mentioned, contains buttons for all open windows and programs. To display a particular program or window, click the button in the taskbar.

The system tray is part of the taskbar and displays the current time as well as status icons. Periodically, a notification message will pop up from the system tray alerting you to events or suggesting actions. For instance, when a print job is successfully printed, you see a printer icon, and then a message noting that the print job is complete. To close a message, click its close button.

Windows XP might also prompt you to check for new updates or to try out certain features (especially MSN Passport, which you can use to get and send Instant Messages). To access one of the highlighted features, click in the message.

## WORKING WITH WINDOWS

Windows XP displays all programs and content in a window on the desktop. When you start a program, for instance, you see the program window. When you open a folder, you see the contents in a window. Part of using Windows, then, is understanding how to manipulate the windows so that you can see and work with the area you want. Review these simple skills for help with working with any kind of window:

- To open a program window, start the program (as covered in Lesson 3). To open a content window, double-click the drive or folder icon or select the folder from the Start menu.
- When a window is open, you see the controls for the window in the upper-right corner. Figure 2.4 shows the My Computer window open. The current window appears on top of any other open windows and the title bar is brighter.
- To close a window, click its **Close** button.
- To minimize a window (shrink it to a taskbar button), click its **Minimize** button.
- To maximize a window so that it fills the entire screen, click its **Maximize** button.

TIP

**Maximized Windows** When a window is maximized it does not have borders; therefore, you cannot move or resize it since it fills the entire screen. Also, the Maximize button changes to a Restore button. You can click the Restore button to return the window to its original size.

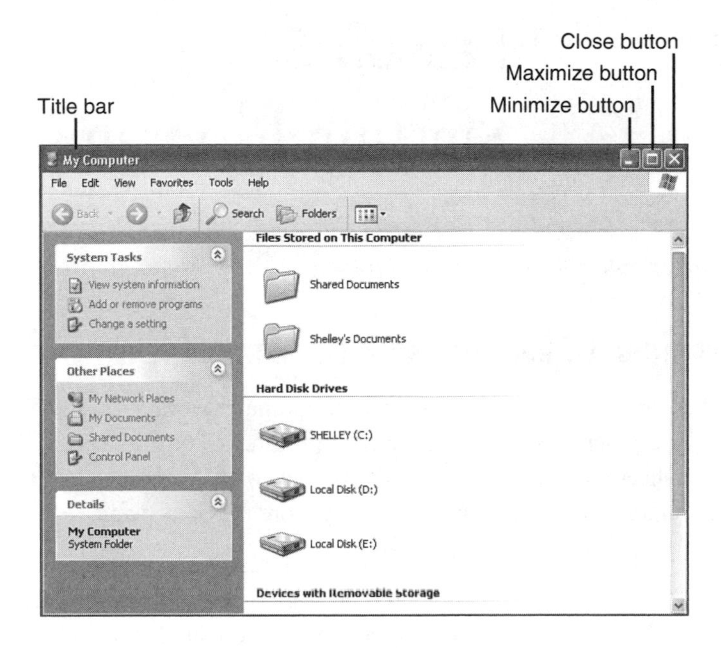


**FIGURE 2.4**

*In the My Computer window you can move, resize, minimize, and close windows as needed.*

- To move a window, put the mouse pointer on the title bar and drag the window to the location you want.
- To resize a window, put the mouse pointer on a border and then drag the border to resize the window.

In this lesson you learned about the Windows XP desktop and how to work with windows. In Lesson 3 you learn how to start and exit programs.

# LESSON 3
# Starting Programs

*In this lesson you learn how to start, switch, and exit programs.*

## STARTING A PROGRAM FROM THE START MENU

You spend most of the time using your computer working in some type of a program—a word processing program to type letters, a spreadsheet program to create budgets, and so on. You can start a program in any number of ways, including from the Start menu.

When you install a new Windows program, that program's installation procedure sets up a program icon (and sometimes a program folder if the program includes several components). These are listed within the Start menu.

You can use one of two methods for using the Start menu. If you commonly use a program and it is listed on the Start menu, you can click it from the left pane of the Start menu. If the program is not listed, you can display all programs.

### STARTING A RECENT PROGRAM

Follow these steps to start a one of your commonly used programs:

1. Click the **Start** button. The left pane displays the last six programs you used.
2. Click the program. That program is started, and you see the program window.

**Change the List** You can change how many programs are listed as well as clear the list. To do so, right-click the **Start** button and select **Properties**. On the Start Menu tab, click **Customize**. In the Customize Start Menu dialog box, select the number of programs to display. To clear the list, click the **Clear List** button, and then click **OK**.

## LISTING ALL PROGRAMS

Follow these steps to start any of the installed programs:

1. Click **Start**, and then click **All Programs**. You see a list of all the program icons and program folders (see Figure 3.1).

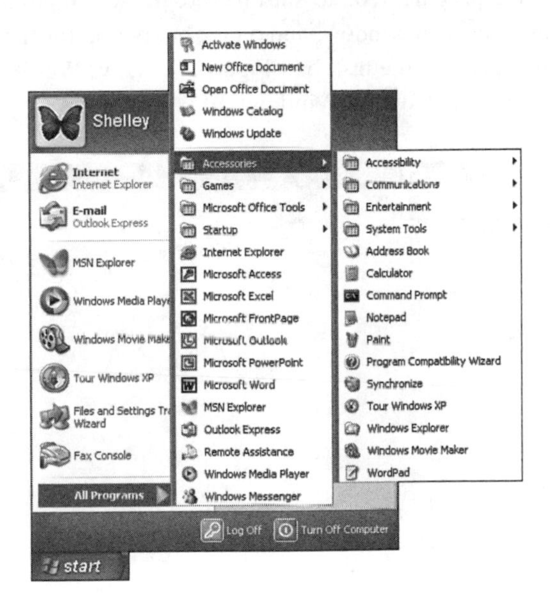


**FIGURE 3.1**
*You can access all of the installed programs by clicking the All Programs button on the Start menu.*

2. If necessary, click the program folder. Any items with an arrow next to them are program folders rather than icons. When you click the program folder, you see the program icons within that folder. For instance, if you click Accessories, you see the Accessory programs included with Windows XP. Follow this step until you see the icon for the program you want to start.

TIP

**Point or Click** To display a folder, you can simply point to it rather than click. If you have trouble getting the folder to stay open, it is easier to click than point.

3. Click the program icon to start the program. The program opens in its own window, and a task bar button for the program appears in the task bar. Figure 3.2 shows WordPad, a program included with Windows XP.

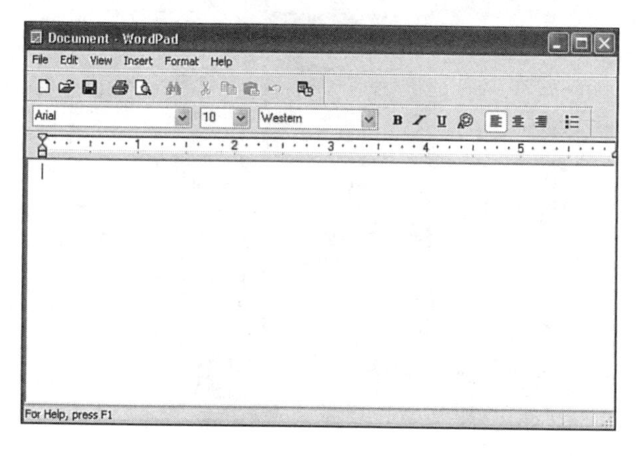


**FIGURE 3.2**

*Most program windows include similar items, making it easy to learn skills in one program that apply to all. For example, nearly all programs include a menu bar, which you can use to select commands.*

## Starting a Program from a Shortcut Icon

In addition to the Start menu, you can also start programs from shortcut icons. Some programs automatically create shortcut icons, placing them on the desktop. You can also add shortcut icons to programs yourself, as covered in Lesson 16, "Setting Up Programs."

To start a program from a shortcut icon, double-click the shortcut icon on the desktop. The program starts and displays in its own window. A task bar button appears for the program.

## Switching Between Programs

You may often work with more than one type of program at the same time. Windows XP enables you to quickly switch from one program to another. For example, you might want to review sales figures in a worksheet while at the same time creating a sales report in a word processing program. Switching between programs enables you not only to view data from several sources, but also to share data among programs.

As mentioned, when you start a program, a button for that program is displayed in the task bar. To switch to another program, simply click the button for that program. That program becomes the active program. For example, in Figure 3.3, Outlook Express is open as well as WordPad. You can tell that WordPad is the current program because its button is darkened. To switch to Outlook Express, click its button on the task bar.

**FIGURE 3.3**
*The task bar buttons display the document and program name for each open program and window.*

## EXITING A PROGRAM

When you finish working in a program, close it to free system memory. Although systems with 128MB or more of system memory can handle several programs open at once, too many can tax your system's memory and slow the computer's processes. You can use one of several methods to close a program:

- Click **File**, and then click the **Exit** command. The program closes.
- Click the **Close** button for the program window.
- Press **Alt+F4**.

**CAUTION**

**Save first!** If you have created a document in the program, make sure you save before you exit. If you have not saved a file and close the program, most applications prompt you to save. To save the document, click **Yes.** To close the document without saving, click **No**. To return to the document without exiting the program, click **Cancel**. See Lesson 4, "Working with Documents," for the important details on saving files.

Now that you have learned how to start programs, turn to the next lesson for information on how to save and display the documents you create with these programs.

# LESSON 4
# Working with Documents

*In this lesson you learn how to save, open, and create documents.*

## SAVING A DOCUMENT

When you work in most programs, you save your work as some type of document—a word processing file such as a memo, a worksheet file such as a budget, a database file such as a list of clients, and so on. One of the most important things you should remember about using a computer is that you need to save your work and save often.

**CAUTION**

**Save Often!** Don't wait until you finish a document before you save it. If the power goes off or the computer gets stuck, you lose all your work if you have not saved. Instead save periodically as you create and edit the document.

When you save your work, the program saves the file in an appropriate file format. The first time you save a file, you must assign that file a name and location. You can include up to 255 characters for the name, including spaces. For the location, you can select any of the drives and folders on your computer.

Follow these steps to save a document:

1. Click **File**, and then click the **Save As** command. You see the Save As dialog box (see Figure 4.1).

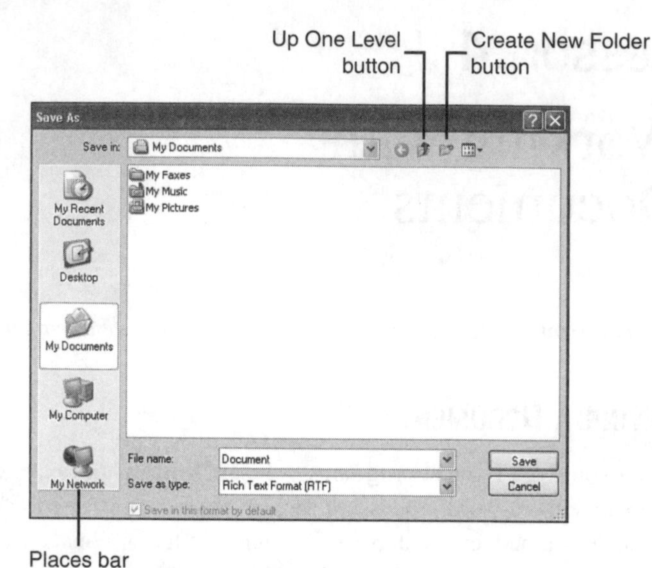


**FIGURE 4.1**
*This is the dialog box for saving in WordPad. The dialog box options may vary from program to program.*

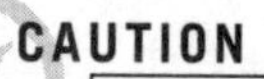

**CAUTION**

**Options May Vary** The steps for saving a document are basically the same regardless of the application you're using. However, some programs offer additional options for saving. For exact directions for your particular program, check that application's manual.

2. Type a name. Some programs suggest a default name. It's best to replace this name with a more descriptive file name.

3. Select the location for the file:

   To save the document in another folder, double-click that folder if it is listed.

To select one of the common folders, click the icon in the Places Bar. For example to open the My Computer folder, click the **My Computer** button.

If the folder is not listed, you can move up through the folder structure by clicking the **Up One Level** button.

To select another drive or folder, display the Save in drop-down list, and then select the drive or folder.

4. Click **Save**. The document is saved, and the title bar displays the name of the document.

After you've saved and named a file, you can click **File** and select **Save** to resave that file to the same location with the same name. When you save again, the disk file is updated to include any changes or additions you made to the file.

**TIP**

**Create a New Folder** You can create a new folder from within the Save As dialog box. To do so, click the **Create New Folder** button, type the new folder name, and press **Enter**.

## Closing a Document

When you are finished working with a document, close it to free up system resources. Most programs, with the exception of WordPad and Paint, include a Close command and a Close button for the document window. To close the document, select **File**, **Close** or click the **Close** button for the document window. In WordPad and Paint you must open another document, create a new document, or exit the program to close the document.

## OPENING A DOCUMENT

As mentioned earlier, when you save a document the information is saved in a file at the location (folder and drive) you selected. When you want to work on that file again—to make changes, to print the file, and so on—you open the file. Follow these steps to open a document:

1. If necessary, start the program you used to create the file.
2. Click **File**, and then click the **Open** command. You see the Open dialog box (see Figure 4.2). If you see the file you want to open, skip to step 4.

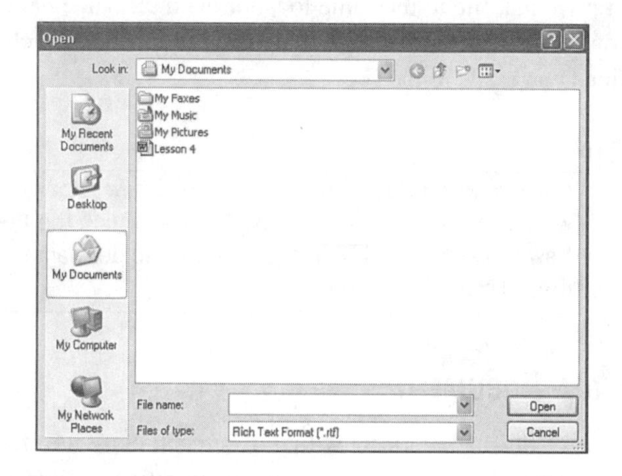


**FIGURE 4.2**
*Use the Open dialog box to display and open the document you want to work with.*

3. If necessary, change to the location where the file was stored by doing any of the following:

   Double-click the folder that contains the file.

   If you don't see the folder listed, click the **Up One Level** button to move up through the folders and display other folders.

To display another drive or folder, display the Look in drop-down list and select the drive or folder.

To display one of the common folders, click its name in the Places bar. For example, to open the My Documents folder, click the **My Documents** button in the Places bar.

4. When you see the file you want to open, double-click its name to open the file. The document is displayed onscreen.

**TIP**

**Can't Find a File?** If you can't find the file you want, it could be because you did not save it where you thought you did. Try looking in a different drive or folder. If you still can't find it, try searching for the file. For more information about searching for files, see Lesson 7, "Finding Files."

## Creating a New Document

When you start most programs, a blank document is displayed. If you use this document and save it, you can always create a new blank document at any time. In addition to blank documents, many programs enable you to select a template on which to base the new document. A *template* is a predesigned document that includes text and formatting. If you don't want a blank document, you can select a template for the new document.

To create a new document, follow these steps:

1. In the program, click **File**, **New**.
2. If you see a New dialog box, click the type of document you want to create, and then click the **OK** button. A new document is displayed. You can use any of the program tools to create and save this new document.

**TIP**

**Creating Documents** For exact instructions on how to use a program to create a document, check the program's documentation. Entering data in most programs is pretty straightforward. For instance, in a word processing program, you just start typing. In a worksheet, you select the cell (intersection of a row and column) and type the entry. Instructions for more complex programs—for instance, a database program—may require more upfront work.

In this lesson you learned the importance of saving your work and also how to redisplay a document you have saved. In Lesson 5, "Using My Computer to Organize Your Folders," you learn how to organize the documents you save into folders.

# LESSON 5
# Using My Computer to Organize Your Folders

*In this lesson you learn how to open My Computer and navigate among the folders on your computer.*

## OPENING MY COMPUTER

My Computer is an icon that represents all of the drives on your system. To open folders and display files, you often start by opening **My Computer**. When you open this window, you can then open any of your drives to see the folders and files contained on that drive.

Why would you want to do so? When you need to open a particular file, you need to find and open the folder that contains that file. For instance, if you want to create a shortcut to a program, you have to first display the program file. When you want to move, copy, or delete files, you start by displaying them. Again, you find and open the folder where the files are stored.

Follow these steps to open My Computer:

1. Click **Start**.
2. Click **My Computer**. You see icons for each of the drives on your computer as well as system folders (see Figure 5.1).

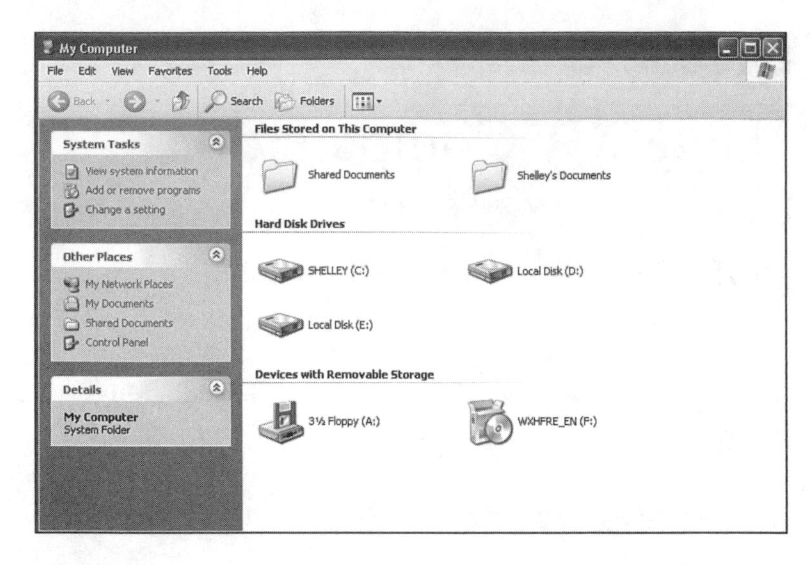


**FIGURE 5.1**
*When you want to work with the folders or files on your computer, you can start with My Computer.*

**Use Shortcut Icon** If you have added the shortcut icon for My Computer to your desktop, you can double-click this icon to open My Computer. See Lesson 2, "Understanding the Windows XP Desktop," for information on adding this icon to your desktop.

To help you keep your documents organized, Windows sets up several special folders in addition to My Computer. These include My Documents, My Pictures, and My Music. You can view the contents of any of these folders by clicking **Start**, and then clicking the folder you want to open.

## Opening Drives and Folders

Two drives nearly all computers have are a floppy drive (drive A:) and a hard drive (drive C:). If you have more than one drive, they are named D:, E:, and so on. If you have a CD drive or a DVD drive, it also is named with a letter. By default, Windows XP groups the drives by type, as shown in Figure 5.1. Opening a hard drive is easy. Just double-click the icon representing the drive you want to open (see Figure 5.2).

**CAUTION**

**Opening a CD/DVD Drive** If you double-click the icon for your CD or DVD drive, Windows may launch an autorun file (if available) or play the first track (for audio CDs). To see the contents of a CD or DVD drive, right-click the drive and choose **Explore**.

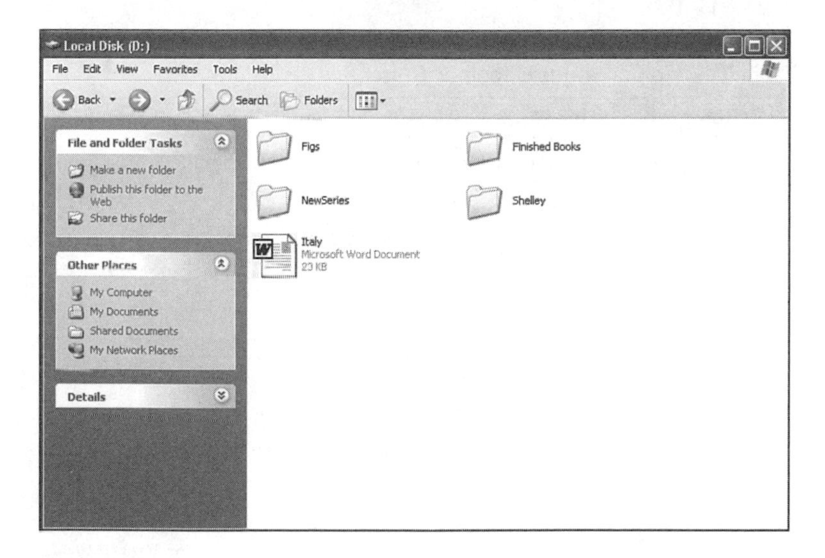


**FIGURE 5.2**

*This figure shows the contents of the hard drive D:. Note the different icons for folders and files.*

Each folder icon represents a folder on your hard drive. Each page icon represents a document (file). The look of the page or document icon varies depending on the program used to operate the document. You can nest folders within folders to organize the contents of your hard drive. To open a folder, double-click its icon. You can continue opening folders until you see the file or folder you want to work with. To close a window, click the **Close** button.

## NAVIGATING FOLDERS

Each folder window includes a toolbar that you can use to navigate from folder to folder. You can go back and forth among previously viewed content windows. You can also move up one level in the folder structure to the containing folder. For instance, you might move up to the desktop level and then open drives and folders to move to another branch of the folder structure. Table 5.1 identifies each toolbar button and its purpose.

**Table 5.1** Folder Window Toolbar Buttons

| Button | Click to... |
|---|---|
|  Back | Go back to a previously viewed folder. |
|  | Return to a previously viewed folder. You can go forward only if you have clicked Back to go back a step. |
|  | Display the next level up in the folder structure. |
|  Search | Display the Search bar to search for a folder or file. See Lesson 7, "Finding Files," for more information. |
|  Folders | Display a hierarchical folder list (similar to Windows Explorer in previous versions of Windows). See the next section, "Using the Folders Bar." |
|  | Change how the contents of the folder are displayed. Lesson 6, "Managing Files," covers changing the view. |

## USING THE TASK PANE

In Windows XP, My Computer also displays a Task pane with common tasks as well as Other Places and a Details area. For instance, if you are viewing folders, you see File and Folder Tasks. If you are viewing picture files, you see Picture Tasks. When you click an icon, you can see information about the icon in the Details area.

## USING THE FOLDERS BAR

If you want to see a hierarchical listing of all the folders on your system instead of the Task pane, you can display the Folders bar. You might prefer this view when working with folders and files because you can see the contents of the selected folder as well as all the other drives and folders on your computer. The Folders bar makes it easier to move and copy by dragging, for instance. Click the **Folders** button to display the Folders bar (see Figure 5.3).

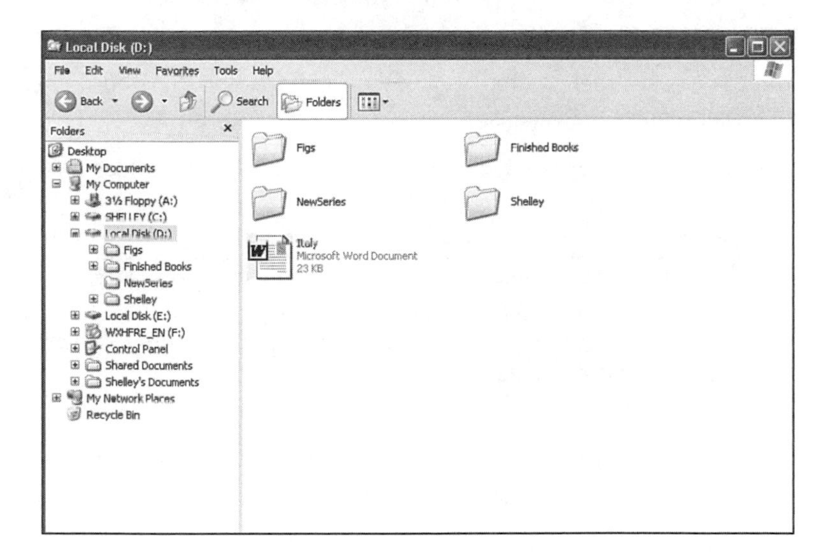


**FIGURE 5.3**

*Displaying the Folders bar lets you view all the drives and folders on your computer.*

The top level is the Desktop; beneath that you see the drives and folders on the desktop. You can expand or collapse any of the folders and drives in the list by clicking the plus sign next to the drive or folder. For instance, click the plus sign next to My Computer. When you click a plus sign to expand the folder or drive, the icon changes to a minus sign. You can click the minus sign to hide the contents of that item. For instance, you might hide content that isn't relevant to the task you are performing. To close the Folders bar, click the Folders button again or click the **Close** button for the bar.

## CREATING A NEW FOLDER

Finding, saving, and opening documents is easier if you group related files into folders. For example, you might want to create a folder for all your word processing documents or for each person that uses your computer. Creating a folder enables you to keep your documents separated from the program's files so that you can easily find your document files.

You can create a folder within any of the existing folders on your computer. Follow these steps:

1. Open the folder in which you want to create the new folder.

TIP

**Use My Documents** Windows XP includes several shortcuts to the My Documents folder. Therefore, you may want to set up all your document folders within this one key system folder.

2. In the Task pane, click **Make a new folder**. The new folder appears in the window and the name is highlighted.
3. Type a new name and press **Enter**. The folder is added.

## WORKING WITH FOLDERS

You can delete, move, rename, and copy folders, much as you do with files (see Lesson 6). The following are some of the key folder tasks:

- To select a folder, click it.
- To delete a folder, select it, and then click **Delete this folder** in the Task pane or press the **Delete** key on your keyboard. Click the **Yes** button to confirm the deletion.
- To copy a folder and its contents, select the folder, and then click **Copy this folder**. In the Copy Items dialog box, select the folder where you want to place the copy (see Figure 5.4). You can expand any of the drives or folders by clicking the plus sign next to the item. Click **Copy**.

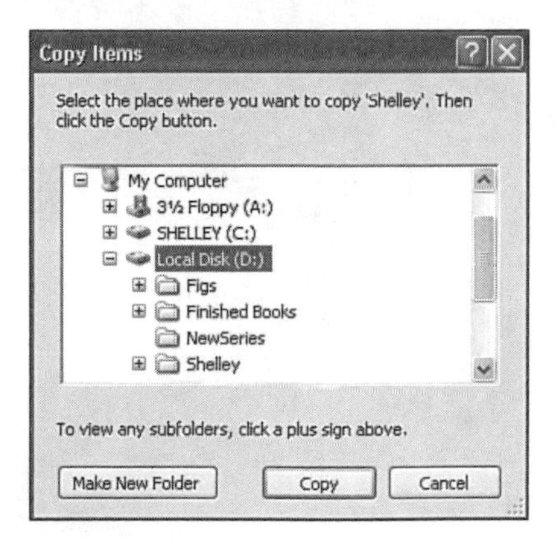


**FIGURE 5.4**
*To copy a folder and its contents, select the drive or folder in which to place the copy.*

- Moving a folder is similar to copying, only when you move a folder the original is deleted and only the moved folder (and its contents) remain. Select the folder, click **Move this folder**, and then select the drive or folder in which to place the folder. The dialog box that appears is similar to the Copy Items dialog box, but is for moving. Click the **Move** button.

- To rename a folder, select the folder and then click the **Rename this folder** link. The current name is selected. Type the new name and press **Enter**.

In this lesson you learned how to view and work with the folders on your system. Turn to Lesson 6 for help on working with the files stored in the folders on your computer.

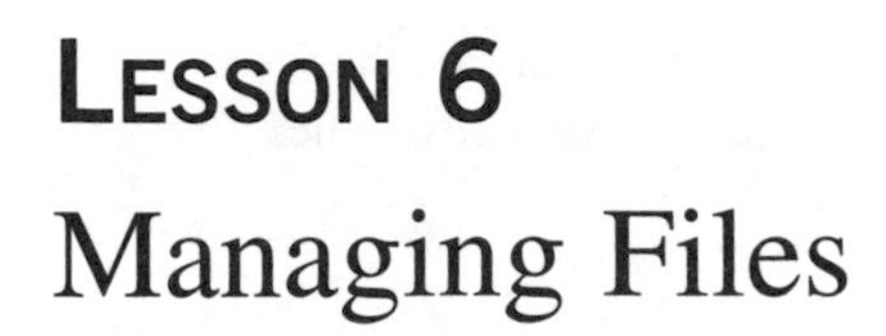

# Lesson 6
# Managing Files

*In this lesson you learn how to work with the files—select, move, copy, delete, and so on—on your computer.*

## Displaying and Selecting Files

When you save the work from a program, that data is saved as a file on the drive and folder you select. You work with these files often. You may need to copy a file or move a file to another folder. You may want to create a shortcut to a file. To start, you open the drive and folder where the file is stored (as covered in Lesson 5, "Using My Computer to Organize Your Folders").

After you display the files you want to work with, select the file or files. You can select a single file or several files. For instance, you may want to delete a group of files.

To select a file or files, do any of the following:

- To select a single file, click it.
- To select several files next to each other, click the first file of the group that you want to select, hold down the **Shift** key, and then click the last file. The first and last files and all files in between are selected.
- To select several files that are not next to each other, hold down the **Ctrl** key and click each file you want to select.
- To select all files, click the **Edit** menu, and then click the **Select All** command (or press Control+A).

- To deselect a file or group of files, click outside the file list. To deselect an individual file in a group, Control+click the file.

## DELETING A FILE

Eventually, your computer becomes full of files, and you have a hard time organizing and storing them all. You can delete any files you no longer need.

Windows XP doesn't really delete a file; instead, it moves the file to the Recycle Bin. If needed, you can retrieve the file from the Recycle Bin.

Follow these steps to delete a file:

1. Select the file(s) you want to delete. Note that the Task pane displays file-related tasks (see Figure 6.1).

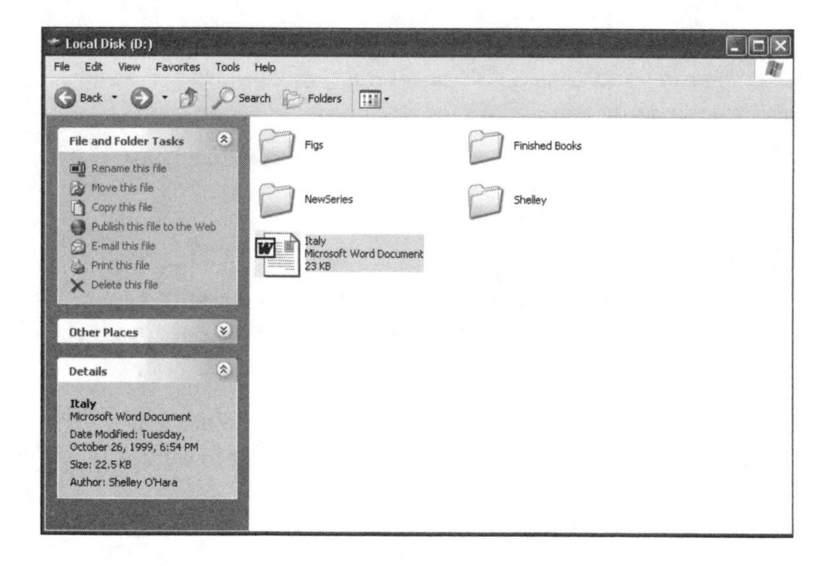


**FIGURE 6.1**
*When you select a file, Windows XP displays tasks relating to files in the Task pane.*

2. Click **Delete this file.**
3. Click **Yes** to confirm the deletion. Windows removes the file(s), placing it (them) in the Recycle Bin.

TIP

**View File Details** When you select a single file, you can view details about the file in the Task pane. If the Details area is not displayed, click the down arrow next to the heading. If you have multiple files selected, this area displays the number of files selected as well as the total file size.

## Undeleting a File

Sometimes you delete a file or folder by mistake. If you make a mistake, you can retrieve the file or folder from the Recycle Bin (as long as the Recycle Bin has not been emptied) and return the file to its original location.

To undelete a file, follow these steps:

1. Double-click the **Recycle Bin icon** on your desktop. You see the contents of the Recycle Bin, including any folders, icons, or files you have deleted (see Figure 6.2).

CAUTION

**Can't Open File** You cannot open files from the Recycle Bin. You can only restore the file to its previous location, move it to another drive or folder, or permanently delete it.

TIP

**Undelete a Folder** Follow these same steps to undelete a folder and its contents. Select the folder, and then click **Restore this item**.

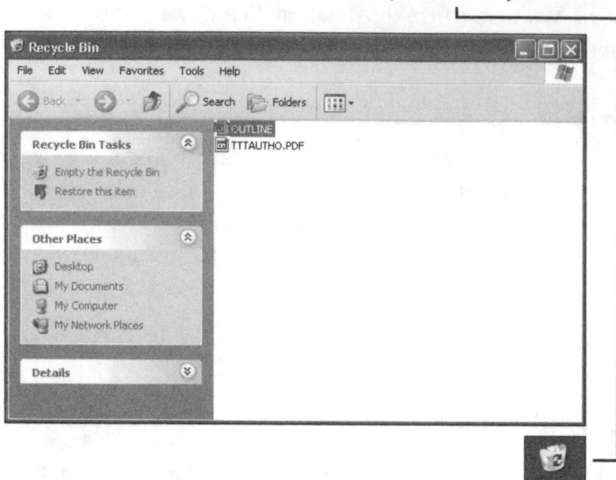


**FIGURE 6.2**
*The Recycle Bin includes any files and folders you have deleted.*

2. Select the file you want to undelete.
3. Click **Restore this item** in the Task pane. The file is moved from the Recycle Bin back to its original location.
4. Click the **Close** button to close the Recycle Bin.

Even though you can't see them in My Computer or File Explorer, the contents of the Recycle Bin take up disk space, so periodically you should empty it. Be sure that it doesn't contain any items you need. Remember Murphy's Law. You'll probably need the file the second you permanently delete it!

After you've checked the contents, you can permanently delete the contents by emptying the Recycle Bin. Double-click the **Recycle Bin icon**. Then click **Empty Recycle Bin** in the Task pane. Windows displays the Confirm Multiple File Delete dialog box; click **Yes** to empty the Recycle Bin.

## Renaming a File

If you did not use a descriptive name when you saved the file or if the current name doesn't accurately describe the file contents, you can rename it. You can rename only a single file at a time. Follow these steps:

1. Select the file you want to rename.
2. Click **Rename this file** in the Task pane. The current name is highlighted.
3. Type the new name and press **Enter**. The file is renamed.

## Copying a File

Windows makes it easy to copy files from one folder to another and from one disk to another. You might copy files to create a backup copy or to revise one copy while keeping the original file intact. Follow these steps to copy a file:

1. Select the file(s) you want to copy.
2. Click **Copy this file** in the Task pane. You see the Copy Items dialog box (see Figure 6.3).

**FIGURE 6.3**

*In this dialog box, expand the drive or folder listing until you see the folder you want. Then click the folder to select it.*

3. Display and then click the folder in which you want to place the file. You can expand the folder listing by clicking the plus sign next to the icon, drive, or folder.
4. Click the **Copy** button. Windows copies the files to the new location.

TIP

**Copying to a Floppy Disk** You might want to copy a file to a floppy disk to take the file with you or to make a backup copy. Windows provides a shortcut (the Send To command) for copying a file to a floppy disk. Insert a disk into the floppy drive, and then select the file(s) to copy. Right-click the file(s) and select the Send To command from the shortcut menu. Click the floppy drive. The files are copied.

## MOVING A FILE

You might need to move files from one folder or drive to another (for example, to reorganize folders by putting similar files together in the same folder). You can also move a file that you accidentally saved in the wrong folder. Moving is similar to copying. Follow these steps:

1. Select the file(s) you want to move.
2. Click **Move this file** in the task pane. You see the Move Items dialog box similar to the Copy Items dialog box shown in Figure 6.3.
3. Display, and then click the folder where you want to place the file. You can expand the folder listing by clicking the plus sign next to the icon, drive, or folder.
4. Click the **Move** button. Windows moves the files to the new location.

In this lesson you learned the key tasks for working with files. In the next lesson you learn how to find files you have misplaced.

# LESSON 7
# Finding Files

*In this lesson you learn the many different ways of finding files that you have misplaced on your computer.*

## VIEWING AND SORTING FILES

Saving a file and not being able to find it again is pretty common. Either you didn't save it to the location you thought, or you cannot remember in which folder you saved it. Sometimes you don't remember the exact file name. One way to find files is to change how they are displayed in the folder window. You can view the contents of a window in a variety of ways. You can also sort the contents so that files are listed in alphabetical order, by date, or by type. A new command in Microsoft Windows XP enables you to group similar files together.

### CHANGING THE VIEW

If you want to see more of a window's contents at one time, you can change the view to List. As another alternative, change to Details view to see more detailed information about the contents (size, name, type, or modification date). You can also select Thumbnails, useful for pictures, or Tiles which show an icon along with file information. Changing the way a window displays its contents can make it easier to find what you need.

To change to a different view, follow these steps:

1. In the window you want to change, click the **View** menu or click the down arrow next to the Views button.
2. Select the view you want. The window displays the contents in that view. Figures 7.1 and 7.2 show the contents in Tiles view, and then in List view.

**FIGURE 7.1**

*The default view for most windows is Tiles. This view shows some basic file information.*

## SORTING FILES

Sort the contents of a folder window so that you can more easily find the folders and files you want. Windows enables you to arrange the contents of a window by name, type, date, and size. All views show the sort, but the change is most apparent in Details view because this view includes columns for size, date, and type.

Follow these steps to sort files:

1. Open the window you want to sort.
2. Click **View**, and then click the **Arrange Icons By** command.
3. Select the sort order you want. Windows sorts the files in the selected order. For example, Figure 7.3 shows the files sorted by modification date. Note the sort column is indicated with faint shading and an icon in the heading.

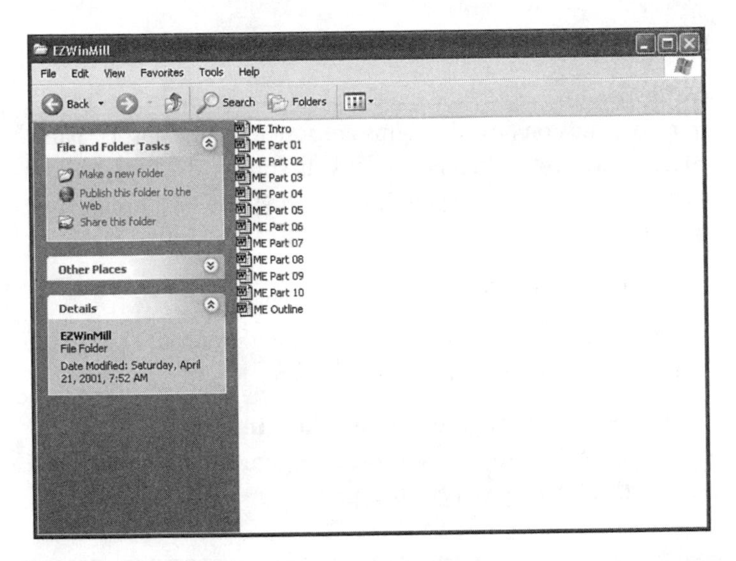


**FIGURE 7.2**

*List view makes it easier to select a group of files because they are listed in order. Also List view takes less room for listing files.*

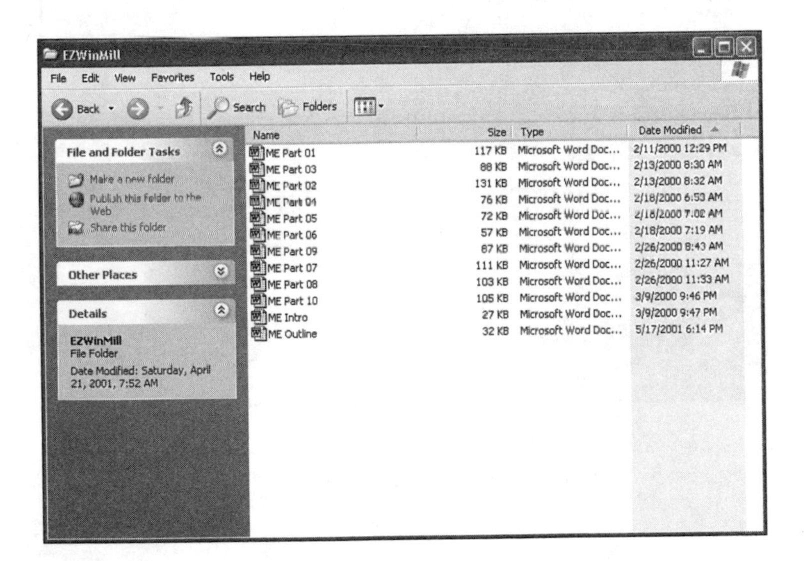


**FIGURE 7.3**

*You can sort files to make it easier to find the file you need.*

## GROUPING FILES

New with Windows XP is the capability to group file icons. The grouping depends on how the items are sorted. If you sort by name, the contents are grouped alphabetically. If you sort by type, the contents are grouped by type. Therefore, sort first and then group. You can group in any view.

Follow these steps to group files:

1. Sort the contents by how you want them grouped. For instance, to group by type, sort by type.
2. Click **View**, **Arrange Icons By**, **Show in Groups**. Windows groups the icons by the sort order. Figure 7.4 shows the files sorted, and then grouped by type.

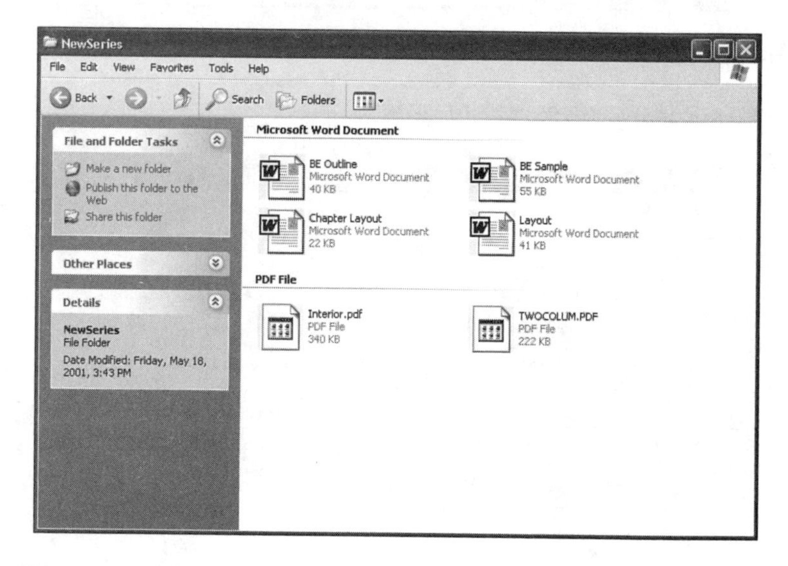


**FIGURE 7.4**
*You can group files to keep similar file types together.*

TIP

**View File Information** Another helpful way to find a file is to view the file details or properties. Select a file, and then expand the Details area in the task pane by clicking the down arrow next to that heading. You see file information. To display file properties, right-click the file, and then select Properties. Some files may have several tabs with identifying information. When you are done reviewing the file properties, click **OK**.

## Searching for Documents

If you have saved a document, but cannot locate it by browsing through your folders, you can search for it. You can search for several different file types. From the search results, you can then open, print, copy, or move the file.

Follow these steps to search for a file:

1. Click the **Start** button, and then click the **Search** command.
2. Select the type of file you want to find. You can search for pictures, music, or video files; documents (word processing, spreadsheet, and so on); or all files and folders.

TIP

**Search the Internet** You can also use the Search command to search the Internet or to search for people (addresses or e-mail information). See Lesson 10, "Browsing the Internet," for more information.

3. Enter the search criteria. The available options vary depending on what you selected to search. Figure 7.5 shows searching for a document. You can specify the last time the file was modified and/or enter all or part of the filename.

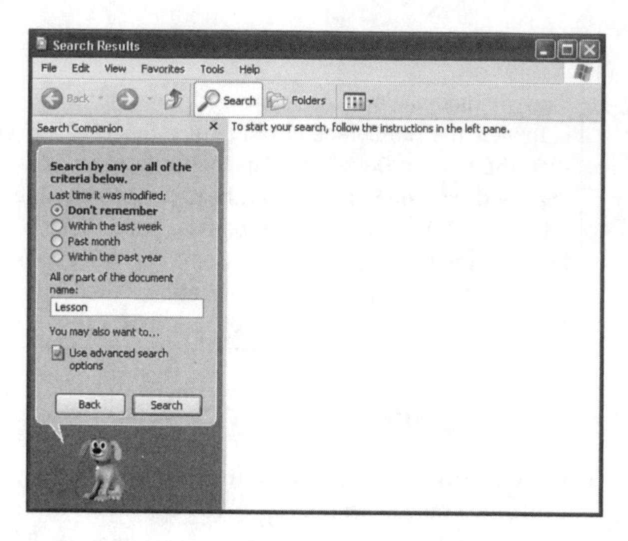


**FIGURE 7.5**
*To search, enter the search criteria that you think will best help Windows XP find a match.*

**TIP**

**Limit Search** To use additional search criteria click the Use advanced search options link. You can then limit the search to a particular drive or folder using the Look in drop-down list. You can also search for a word or phrase in the document.

4. Click the **Search** button. Windows searches and displays a list of found files in the right pane of the window (see Figure 7.6). You can double-click any of the listed files or folders to open that file or folder.

**TIP**

**Search Again** The Search bar lists the number of files found as well as options for refining the search. If the results did not turn up the file you want, search again.

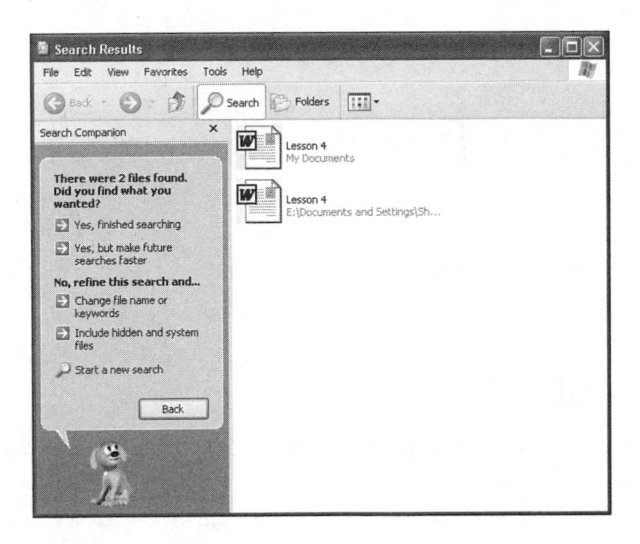


**FIGURE 7.6**

*The results of the search are displayed in the right pane of the Search Results window. You can open, move, copy, or delete any of the listed files.*

5. To close the search window, click its **Close** button.

In this lesson you learned about the many tools you can use to locate a file that has been misplaced. The next lesson discusses printing.

# Lesson 8
# Printing

*In this lesson you learn how to set up a printer, set printer preferences, and print a document.*

## Adding a Printer

In many cases, Microsoft Windows can automatically set up your printer after you attach it. After you plug in the printer, Windows XP initiates the process and alerts you that the printer has been found and installed with messages that pop up from the system tray.

If the automatic setup doesn't work for some reason, you can add a new printer to your Windows setup using a step-by-step guide called a *wizard*. This may occur if you have a newer printer that is not yet added to Windows XP's printer driver list or a really old printer that Windows does not support out of the box.

> **Wizard** A feature that leads you step-by-step through a particular process. For instance, the Add Printer Wizard helps you add a new printer to your setup. You can also find wizards for setting up your fax, e-mail, programs, and other features.

Follow these steps to set up a new printer using the Add Printer Wizard:

1. Click **Start**, and then click **Control Panel**.
2. Click **Printers and Other Hardware**.
3. Click **Add a printer** to start the Add Printer Wizard (see Figure 8.1).

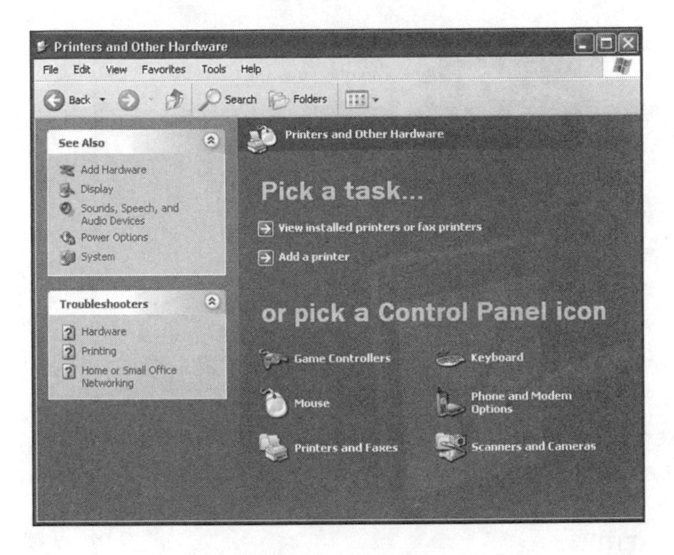


**FIGURE 8.1**

*Use the Printers and Other Hardware Control Panel to install a new printer.*

**TIP**

**Troubleshoot Printer Problems** If you are having problems with your printer, click **Printing** under the Troubleshooters area in the Task pane. This starts Windows XP Troubleshooter which asks you to identify the problem, and then suggests remedies.

4. Complete each step in the wizard, clicking **Next** to move from step to step. You can expect to select the type of printer (local or network), automatic detection or manual setup, the port to which the printer is attached, the printer manufacturer and printer name, printer sharing options, and whether to print a test page. The final step of the wizard lists all your selections (see Figure 8.2).

5. Click **Finish** to finish the printer setup. The printer is set up and added to Windows XP.

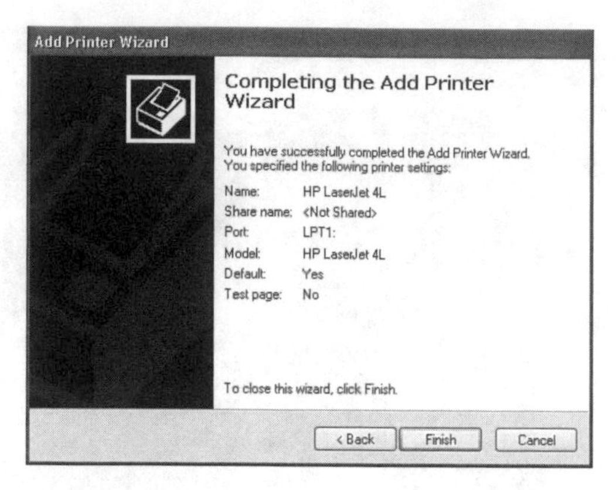


**FIGURE 8.2**
*When you finish all the answers to the wizard, all your selections are listed.*

TIP

**Use Printer Disk** If you have the printer disk with the printer driver file (the file that tells Windows the details of that particular printer), click **Have Disk** on the Install Printer Software wizard page, insert the disk, and then select the drive to search for the file.

TIP

**Go Back a Step** Click the **Back** button in a wizard dialog box to return to the previous dialog box and review or modify your selections.

## SETTING PRINTING PREFERENCES AND PROPERTIES

If you want to modify a printer's settings, start by opening the **Printers and Faxes Control Panel**. You can then view and change the preferences and properties for any of the printers. You can also access the print queue to pause, restart, or cancel a print job.

Printing preferences are settings such as the order pages are printed (beginning to end of document, or end to beginning), orientation (portrait or landscape), and paper source. If you always print a certain way, you can change these settings.

## Viewing Installed Printers

To make any changes, you first must display the printer icon. Follow these steps:

1. Click the **Start** button, and then choose **Control Panel**.
2. Click the **Printers and Other Hardware** category.
3. Click the **Printers and Faxes Control Panel** icon. You see a list of all the installed printers and faxes (see Figure 8.3).

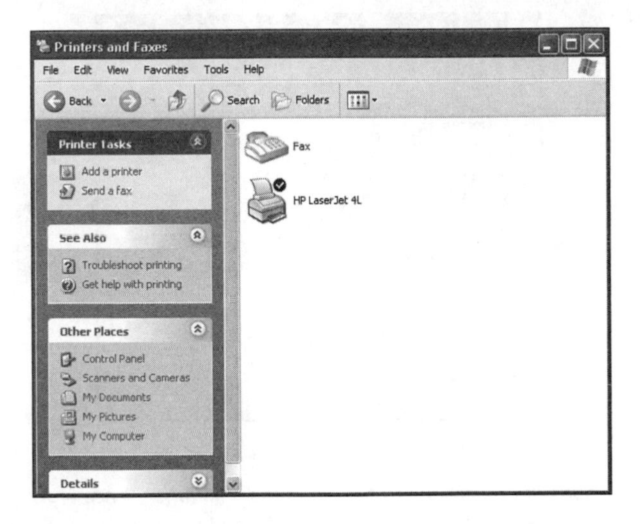


**FIGURE 8.3**
*You can view the installed printers when you want to modify the settings or view the print queue.*

**TIP**

**Default Printer** The default printer is indicated with a check mark. To select another printer as the default, right-click the icon for that printer and select **Set as Default Printer**.

## CHANGING PRINTING PREFERENCES

Changing the printer's preferences changes them for all documents you print on this printer. If you want to change settings for just one document, change the setting in that document instead. To change the printing preferences for all print jobs, follow these steps:

1. Display the printer icon. See the previous section, "Viewing Installed Printers."
2. Select the printer you want to modify.
3. Click **Select printing preferences** in the Task pane. You see the Printing Preferences dialog box (see Figure 8.4).

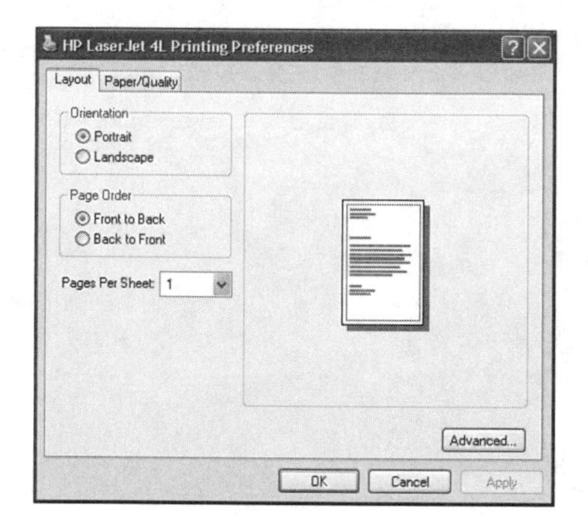


**FIGURE 8.4**
*Use the options in this dialog box to control the orientation, page order, and paper source for all print jobs printed with this printer.*

4. On the Layout tab, select a default orientation and a default page order.
5. Click the **Paper/Quality** tab. Select a default paper source.
6. Click **OK**.

In addition to printing preferences, you can also view and change printer properties. These are more technical details of how your printer works. For example, when the printer is available, the port to which the printer is attached, whether printer sharing is enabled, and other options. To make these changes, select the printer and then click **Set printer properties** in the Task pane. Make any changes to any of the tabs, and then click **OK**.

## PRINTING A DOCUMENT

Printing your documents gives you a paper copy you can proofread, use in reports, give to co-workers, and so on. The options for printing vary from program to program, but the basic steps are the same.

TIP

**Preview First** Most programs enable you to preview a document to check the margins, heads, graphics placement, and so on before you print. Previewing can save time and paper because you can make any needed adjustments before you print. Click **File** and select the **Print Preview** command. After you finish viewing the preview, click the **Close** button.

To print a document, follow these steps:

1. Click **File**, and then click the **Print** command. As a shortcut, look for a Print button in the program's toolbar or use the shortcut key combination (usually Control+P). If you use the command, you see the Print dialog box shown in Figure 8.5. If you use the Print button or shortcut key, the document is printed to the default printer without displaying the dialog box.
2. Make any changes to the print options. Most programs enable you to select a printer, select what is printed (a particular page range, for example), and select the number of copies to

print. Note that the available options vary from program to program.

3. Click the **OK** button. The document is printed.

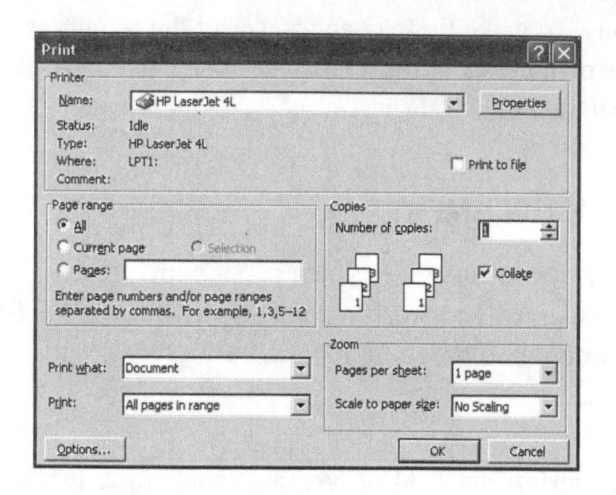


**FIGURE 8.5**
*This figure shows the Print dialog box for Word. Depending on the program you are printing from, you may see different options.*

## VIEWING AND CANCELING PRINT JOBS

The print queue lists the documents that have been sent to a printer, and it shows how far along the printing is. Using the print queue, you can pause, restart, or cancel print jobs. For instance, you may need to pause a print job to change paper. You may cancel a print job that you started by mistake.

Follow these steps to make changes to a print job in progress:

1. Display the printer icon. See the section "Viewing Installed Printers" earlier in this lesson.

2. Select the printer you want to view and click **See what's printing** in the Task pane. You see the print queue (see Figure 8.6). You can also display the print queue by

double-clicking the Printer icon in the system tray of the taskbar (on the far-right side). The Printer icon appears whenever you are printing a document.

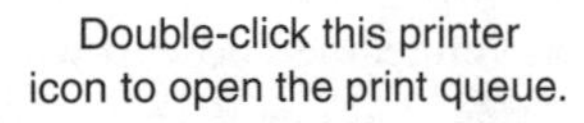


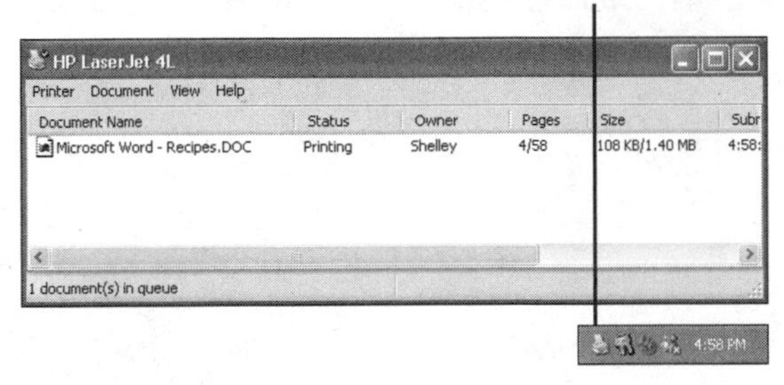


**FIGURE 8.6**
*Use the print queue to pause, restart, or cancel a print job.*

**CAUTION**

**Print Queue Empty** If the print queue window is empty, either the print job never made it to the queue or it was already processed by the printer. Short print jobs are printed quickly, so you might not have time to stop the job.

3. Do any of the following:

   To cancel all print jobs, click **Printer**, and then click the **Cancel All Documents** command. Click **Yes** to confirm the cancellation.

   To pause printing, click **Printer**, and then click **Pause Printing**. To restart after pausing, click **Printer**, and then click **Pause Printing** again.

   To cancel, pause, resume, or restart a particular print job, click the print job in the list. Then click **Document** and select the appropriate command (**Pause**, **Resume**, **Restart**, or **Cancel**).

4. Click the **Close** button to close the queue.

In this lesson you learned how to work with printers. The next lesson covers how to use Outlook Express, the e-mail program included with Windows XP.

# LESSON 9
# Sending E-mail

*In this lesson you learn how to use Outlook Express, the e-mail program included with Windows XP, to send and receive electronic messages (or e-mail).*

## SETTING UP YOUR E-MAIL ACCOUNT

Before you can use Outlook Express, you need to set up your Internet connection and e-mail account information. After you have set up a mail account, you can use Outlook Express to create, send, and receive e-mail over the Internet.

The first time you start Outlook Express you are prompted to set up your e-mail account. You should have handy all the connection information from your Internet and e-mail provider, including your username, e-mail address, password, and technical information such as the incoming mail server name (called the POP3, IMAP, or HTTP server) and the outgoing mail server (called the SMTP server). If you have problems or questions about this information, contact your Internet service provider (often referred to as your ISP).

**TIP**

**Add More Accounts** If you have multiple e-mail accounts, you can set them up and check all mail accounts from Outlook Express. Click **Tools**, and then click the **Accounts** command. Any existing accounts are listed. Click the **Add** button and select **Mail** to start the Internet Connection Wizard. Follow the same steps for setting up the first account, entering your username, password, and so on.

## CHECKING YOUR E-MAIL

After your e-mail account is set up, you can start Outlook Express and check your mail. Follow these steps:

1. Click **Start**, and then click **E-mail** (Outlook Express).
2. If prompted, connect to your Internet service provider. Outlook Express starts and checks your e-mail server for any messages. Messages are then downloaded to Outlook Express. The number of new messages appears in parentheses next to the Inbox in the Folders list. The message header pane lists all messages. Messages in bold have not yet been read. You can open and read any message in the message list (see Figure 9.1).

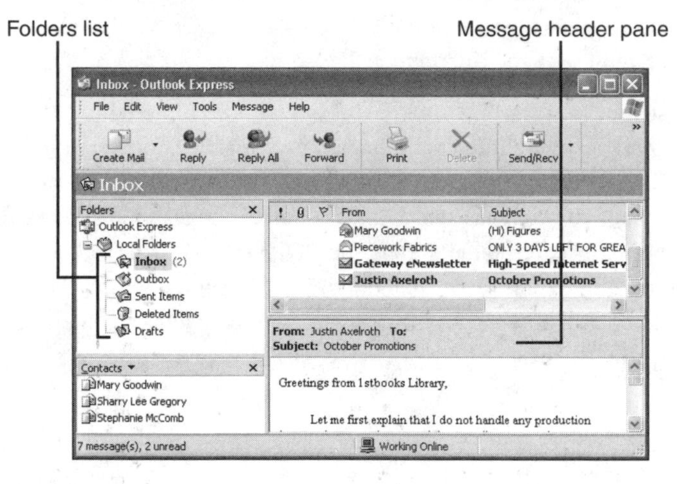


**FIGURE 9.1**
*Start Outlook Express, and then check your Inbox for new messages.*

3. If necessary, in the Folders list of the Outlook Express window, select **Inbox**.
4. Double-click the message you want to read. The message you selected is displayed in its own window (see Figure 9.2).

You can display the previous or next message in the list with the Previous and Next buttons in the toolbar. To close the message, click the **Close** button.

**TIP**

> **Change the Default** By default, Outlook Express displays Outlook Today, an overview of e-mail, newsgroups, and contacts. To go directly to your Inbox when opening Outlook Express, check the option **When Outlook Express starts, go directly to my Inbox** in the Outlook Express window.

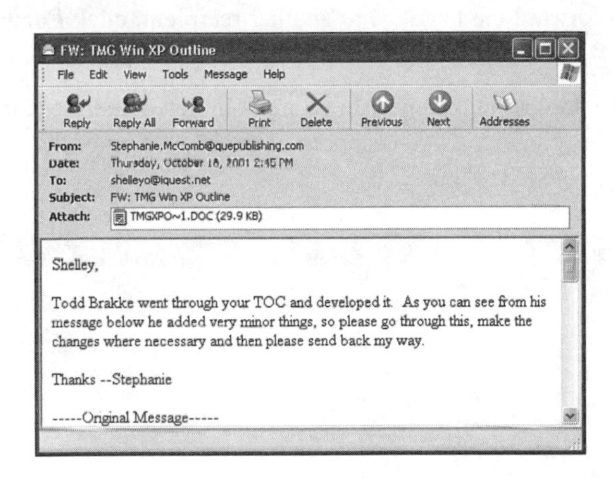


**FIGURE 9.2**

*You can open and review any of the messages you receive. Use the toolbar buttons to display other messages.*

## Responding to Mail

You can easily respond to a message you've received. Outlook Express completes the address and subject lines for you and also includes the text of the original message. You can then type your response. You can reply to just the original sender or to the sender and any other recipients (anyone listed in the Cc: field in the message). You can also forward the message to someone else.

To reply to a message you have received, follow these steps:

1. Display the message to which you want to reply.
2. Do any of the following:

   To reply to just the sender, click the **Reply** button in the toolbar.

   To reply to the sender and any other recipients, click **Reply All**.

   To forward the message to another recipient, click **Forward**. Then type the e-mail address for that person.

   The address and subject lines are completed and the text of the original message is appended to the bottom of the reply message (see Figure 9.3).

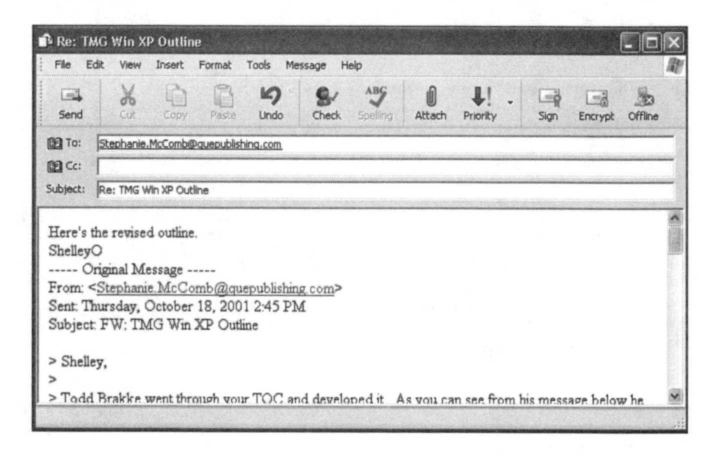


**FIGURE 9.3**
*You can respond to a message by typing a reply, and then sending the message.*

3. Type your message.
4. Click the **Send** button located in the message's toolbar. The message is placed in your Outbox.

Depending on your e-mail preferences, the message may be sent immediately or may be placed in the Outbox and sent when you click the **Send/Rec** button. Also, by default, Outlook Express saves a copy of all sent messages in the Sent Items folder. You can view this folder by clicking **Sent Items** in the Folders bar. To change your e-mail preferences, use the Tools, Options command.

## Creating and Sending New Mail

You aren't limited to replying to existing messages. You can send a message to anyone with an Internet e-mail address. To do so, you must know that person's e-mail address. You can type it or select it from an address book. (See "Getting More from E-mail" later in this lesson.) In addition to the address, you can type a subject and the message.

Follow these steps to create and send a new mail message:

1. In the Outlook Express window, click the **Create Mail** button. You see a blank e-mail message (see Figure 9.4).

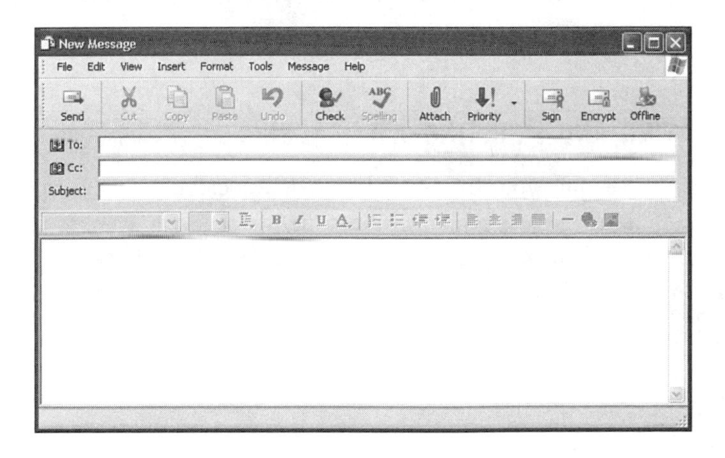


**FIGURE 9.4**
*Create a new e-mail message, and then complete the To: and Subject: fields and type the message.*

2. Type the recipient's address. Addresses are in the format `username@domainname.ext` (for example, `sohara@msn.com`). Press **Tab**.

3. To send a carbon copy (Cc:) to another recipient, type an address for that person and press **Tab**. To skip the Cc: field, simply press **Tab** again.

**CAUTION**

**Wrong Address** If you enter an incorrect address and the message is not sent, you most likely will receive a Failure to Deliver notice. You can then check and correct the address and resend the message.

4. Type a subject in the Subject: text box, and then press **Tab**.

5. Type your message.

6. Click the **Send** button. Like replying to a message, the message is either sent immediately or placed in your Outbox and sent when you click **Send/Rec**, as determined by your e-mail preferences.

## DELETING AND PRINTING MESSAGES

As part of keeping your Inbox uncluttered, you can delete messages. In the Outlook Express window, select the message you want to delete. Or open the message you want to delete. Click the **Delete** button [Delete]. When you delete a message, it is not deleted, but moved to the Deleted Items folder.

**TIP**

**Undelete a Message** To undelete a message, open the Deleted Items folder, select the message, and then move it to another folder by dragging it from the message header pane to one of the folders in the Folders list.

To print an open message, select the message from the Outlook Express window or open the message. Then click the **Print** button Print.

## Exiting and Disconnecting

To exit Outlook Express, click the **Close** button for the program window. If you are prompted to log off, select **Yes** or **Disconnect**. If you are not prompted, right-click the connection icon in the taskbar and select **Disconnect**.

## Getting More from E-mail

The basics of sending e-mail have been covered, but there is plenty more that you can do with Outlook Express. Some other highlights worth investigating are covered in this section.

### Attaching a File to a Message

You can attach a file to send with the message. For example, you can send photographs or if you work from home, you can attach documents such as a report or an expense worksheet. To attach a file, click the **Attach** button in the e-mail message window. Select the file to attach from the Insert Attachment dialog box, and then click the **Attach** button. The file attachment is listed in the Attach text box. Click the **Send** button to send the message and file attachment.

### Opening a File Attachment

If someone sends you a file attachment, you can either open it or save it to disk. Messages with file attachments are indicated with a paper clip icon. Note that to open the attachment, you must have a program that can open and display that particular file type.

Follow these steps:

1. Double-click the message. The file attachment(s) are listed in the Attach text box.
2. Double-click the attachment icon. You see the Open Attachment Warning dialog box (see Figure 9.5).

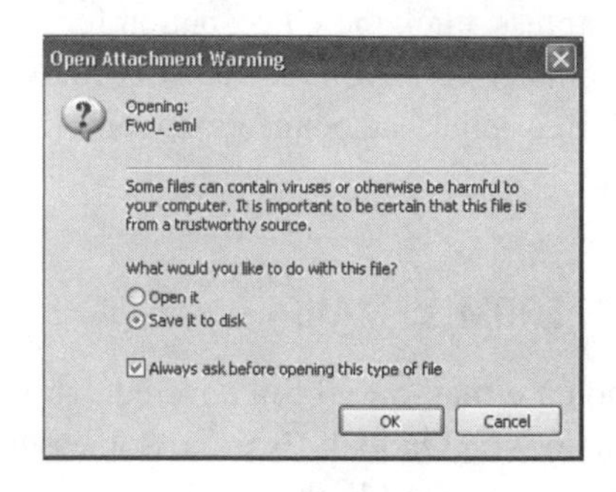


**FIGURE 9.5**
*Handling e-mail attachments.*

3. Select **Open** it or **Save it to disk**.

If you selected to open it, the file is displayed in the associated program (usually the program used to create the file). If you select to save the attachment, you see the Save Attachment As dialog box. Type a filename, select a folder, and click **OK** to save the attachment. (See Lesson 4, "Working with Documents," for more information on saving files.)

## USING THE ADDRESS BOOK

If you often send e-mail to certain people, don't type the address each time. Instead, you can add the name to your Address Book. Then you can quickly select this name and address when creating new messages or forwarding messages.

The fastest way to add an address is to pick it up from an existing message. Display a message to or from the person you want to add.

Then right-click the e-mail address. In the menu that appears, click **Add to Address Book**. The Summary tab displays the default name and e-mail address (see Figure 9.6). Click the **Name** tab and make any changes to the display name (the name that appears in the list). Click **OK** to add the name.

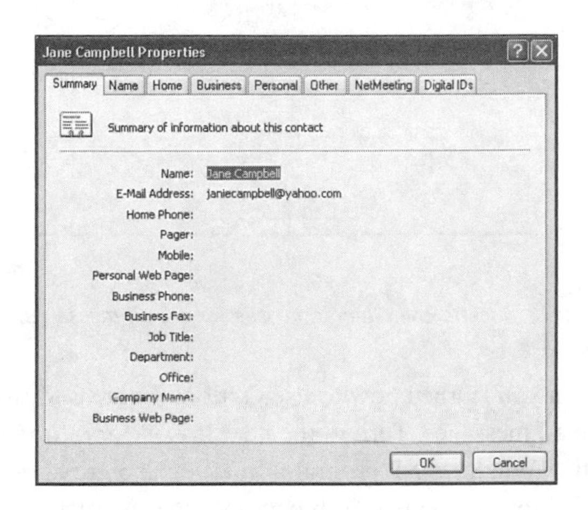


**FIGURE 9.6**
*Add frequently used e-mail addresses to your address book.*

To enter a name, rather than type it, click the **To:** button in a message window. You see the Select Recipients dialog box listing contacts in your Address Book (see Figure 9.7). Select the person to add and click **To:**. That person is added to the Message recipients list. Follow the last step for each person to which you want to send the message. Click **OK**.

**TIP**

**Add Cc: or Bcc:** You can also click names and add them to the carbon copy list (Cc:) or the blind carbon copy (Bcc:). To do so, click the name and then click **Cc:** or **Bcc:**. The carbon copy address is listed. With a blind carbon copy, the recipient receives the message, but the address is not included in the main recipient's message.

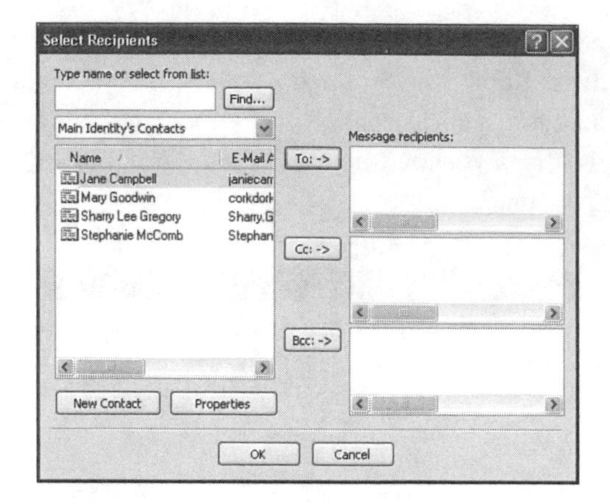


**FIGURE 9.7**
*Use your Address Book to complete addresses for e-mail messages.*

In this lesson you learned how to use Outlook Express to send and receive e-mail messages. Turn to the next lesson for information on using another Windows XP program, Internet Explorer. You can use this Internet browser to view Web pages on the Internet.

# LESSON 10

# Browsing the Internet

*In this lesson you learn how to use Internet Explorer, the Web browser included with Microsoft Windows XP.*

## SETTING UP YOUR INTERNET CONNECTION

If you have a modem and an Internet connection, you can use Internet Explorer to explore the Internet. You can use Internet Explorer to view World Wide Web pages, to search for specific topics, and to set privacy and security features to ensure safe browsing.

To explore the Internet, you must have a modem (analog, cable, DSL or satellite) and an Internet connection. You can get this connection through online providers such as America Online or MSN, or you can get an account from an independent Internet service provider (ISP). Before you can take advantage of all the benefits of the Internet, you must set up your Internet connection. The specifics of setting up depend on your type of connection and your provider. Therefore, follow the specific instructions you received from your Internet provider. You can use the Internet Connection Wizard to do so. Click **Start**, **All Programs**, **Accessories**, **Communications**, **New Connection Wizard**.

**TIP**

**High Speed Access** The slowest form of Internet access is with an analog modem and phone line. Newer, faster methods are becoming more popular and easier to get (and also less expensive than when these features were first introduced). For instance, you can connect with a cable modem and an account with your cable provider. You can also get other special types of service. DSL works over normal phone lines, but requires you to be located near a telco switch box, while a satellite connection works without the need for wires, but is not quite as fast as cable or DSL. You can also get special types of phone lines such as ISDN. If you do not have an Internet account, look into all your options before you decide.

## STARTING INTERNET EXPLORER

After. See Internet Explorer; you've set up your Internet connection, you can start Internet Explorer. Follow these steps:

1. Click **Start**, and then click **Internet**.
2. Enter your username and password (some information might have been completed for you), and then click the **Connect** button. Windows connects to your ISP and displays the Internet Explorer window. You see your start page, usually the MSN home page (see Figure 10.1).

**CAUTION**

**Trouble Connecting?** If you have problems connecting—the line is busy, for example—try again. If you continue to have problems, check with your ISP.

The Internet Explorer window provides several tools for browsing. These are described in Table 10.1.

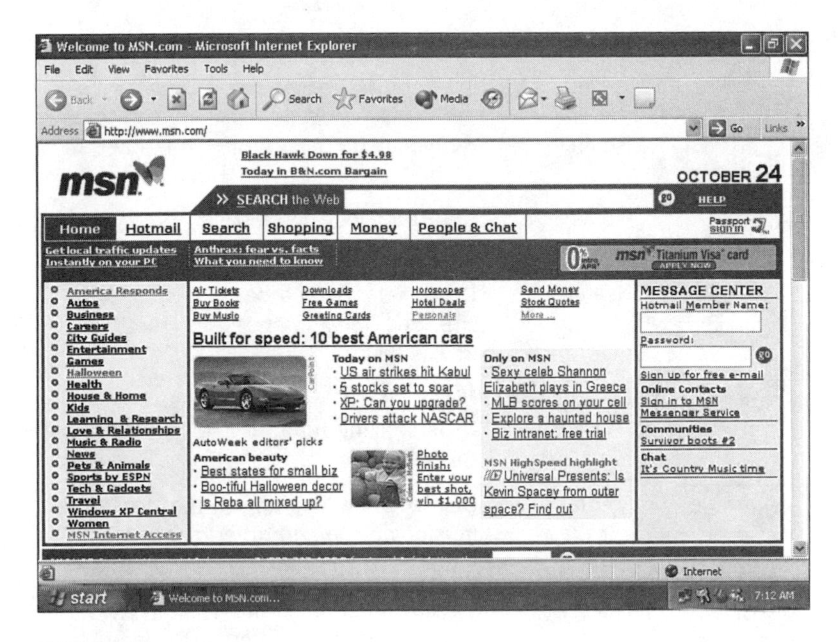


**FIGURE 10.1**

*You can use Internet Explorer to browse the Internet. Take a few minutes to familiarize yourself with the program tools.*

**Table 10.1** Internet Explorer Tools

| Button | Name | Click To... |
|---|---|---|
| Back | Back | Go to the last page you visited. |
| | Forward | Go forward a page. This button is only available if you have clicked **Back** to go back a page. |
| | Stop | Stop the display of a page. Use this button if the page is taking too long to display or if you change your mind. |

**Table 10.1** (continued)

| Button | Name | Click To... |
|---|---|---|
| | Refresh | Redisplay the page, refreshing the data on that page. |
| | Home | Return to your home page. |
| Search | Search | Display the Search bar to search for a site. See "Searching the Internet" later in this lesson. |
| Favorites | Favorites | Display a list of favorite sites. See "Customizing Internet Explorer" later in this lesson. |
| Media | Media | Display a Media guide with access to music, videos, and other media features. |
| | History | Display a list of recently visited sites. See "Customizing Internet Explorer" later in this lesson. |
| | Mail | E-mail a page or link to a page. For more information on e-mail messages, see Lesson 9, "Sending E-mail." |
| | Print | Print the current Web page. |
| | Edit | Open the page in a Web editing program. |
| | Discuss | Join a discussion server for sharing comments about different topics. |
| Links » | Links Bar | Display links to Windows-related sites. |
| Address http://www.msn.com/ Go | Address Bar | Type the address to another Web site. |

TIP

**More Information on Web Publishing** If you are interested in Web publishing, try one of Que's many guides to this topic including ***10 Minute Guide to Microsoft FrontPage 2002***.

## Using Links to Navigate

Information on the Internet is easy to browse because documents contain links to other pages, documents, and sites. You can click a link on the current page to view the page associated with that link. Sometimes the link takes you to another section in the current page or to another page at the current Web site. Other times, clicking a link takes you to an entirely different site. Half the fun of browsing is exploring all types of topics and levels of information using links.

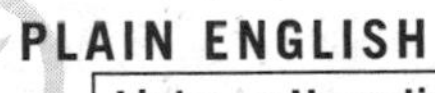

PLAIN ENGLISH

**Links or Hyperlinks** Links are also called *hyperlinks* and usually appear underlined and sometimes in a different color. Images can also be links. You can tell when text or an image is a link because when you point to it, the pointer changes to a hand with a pointing finger, and the address to that link appears in the status bar.

To go to a link, simply click it. You can jump from link to link until you find the information you want. If you get too far astray, remember that you can use the Back button to return to the previous page. You can click the **Back** button as many times as needed to return several pages back. You can also click the down arrow next to the Back button and select the site from the list.

## TYPING A WEB ADDRESS

Typing a site's address is the fastest way to get to that site.

**PLAIN ENGLISH**

**Web Address or URL** You may hear a Web address referred to as a URL (uniform resource locator). Web addresses consist of the protocol (usually **http://**), the Web indicator (usually **www**), and the domain name (something like **nba.com**). So the complete name would be **http://www.nba.com**. You don't have to type the **http://** part when entering an address. Sometimes you can also skip the **www** part. The domain name might also include a path (a list of folders) to the document.

You can find addresses in advertisements, newspaper or magazine articles, and other media sources. The extension (usually **.com**, **.net**, **.gov**, **.edu**, or **.mil**) indicates the type of site (commercial, network resources, government, educational, or military, respectively).

**TIP**

**Try Guessing** Most Web site names are some form of the site or company name, so often you can simply guess. For instance, to go to the NFL site, type **www.nfl.com**. If the address is incorrect, you'll see a page explaining the site is not available or you may inadvertently find that someone else has registered that address for some other purpose. You can try another version of the name or search for the site as covered in "Searching the Internet" later in this lesson.

To go to an address, follow these steps:

1. Click in the **Address** bar.
2. Type the address of the site you want to visit, and then press **Enter**. Internet Explorer displays the page for that address.

TIP

**Use AutoComplete** If you have typed a specific address before, you only need to type its first few letters and Internet Explorer will display the rest. Press **Enter** to let Internet Explorer complete the address for you.

## Searching the Internet

The Internet includes many different sites. Looking for the site you want by browsing can be like looking for the proverbial needle in the haystack. Instead, you can search for a topic and find all sites related to that topic.

To search for sites on a particular topic, follow these steps:

1. Click the **Search** button in the toolbar. You see the Search bar in the right pane of the Internet Explorer window.
2. Type what you want to find and then click the **Search** button (see Figure 10.2).

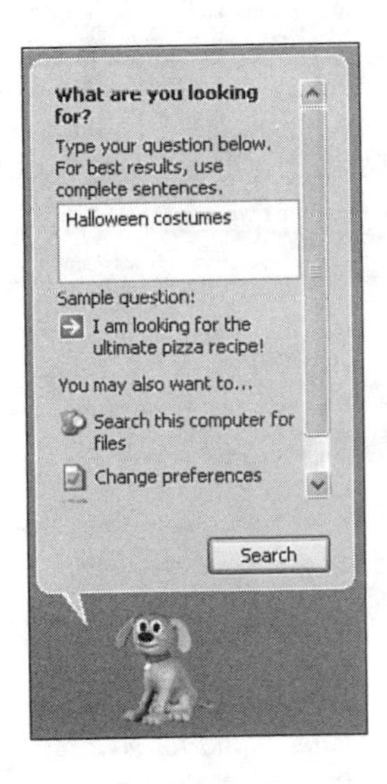


**FIGURE 10.2**
*Type the topic that you want to match into the Search Companion.*

TIP

**Saying Bye-Bye to the Animated Dog** Some people like the animated characters Microsoft has a tendency to include in its programs. Others find them annoying. To turn off the character, click **Turn off animated character** in the Search bar. You may have to scroll through the Search bar to see this option, which is listed last.

You see the results of the search in the window on the right (see Figure 10.3). You can scroll through the list to see information about the first set of matches. If more than one page of matches is found, you can click the **Next** link to display the next set of matches. To go to any of the found sites, click the link in the search results window. The page you selected appears in the right pane.

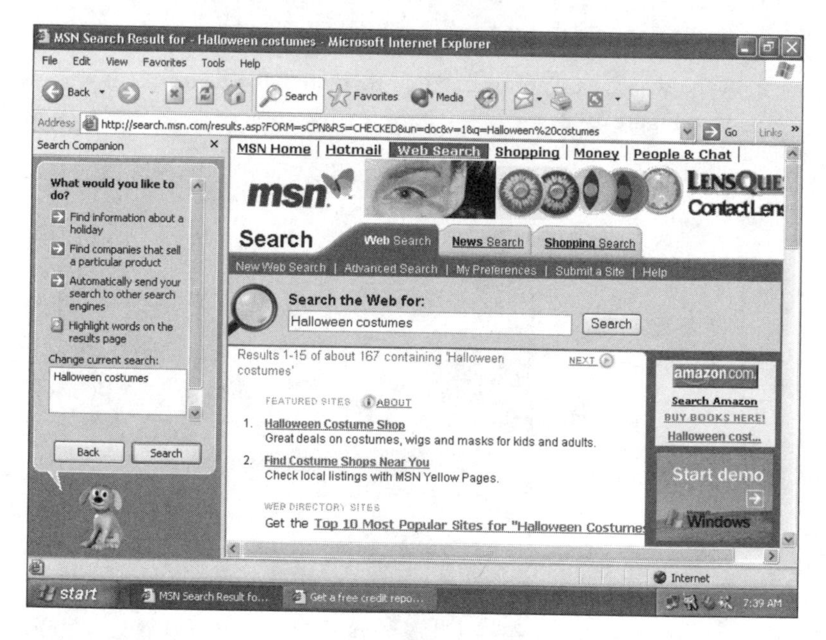


**FIGURE 10.3**

*You can review all of the matches found for your topic. You can also refine the search using suggestions in the Search bar.*

If you don't find an appropriate match, you can refine your search. The Search bar (see the left pane in Figure 10.3) provides some suggestions for fine-tuning the search. To close the Search bar, click its **Close** button or click the **Search** button again.

## Customizing Internet Explorer

To make browsing even easier, you can use any number of shortcuts and customization features of Internet Explorer. This section highlights just a few.

### Setting Up a Favorites List

If you find a site that you especially like, you might want a quick way to return to it without having to browse from link to link or having to remember the address. Fortunately, Internet Explorer enables you to build a list of favorite sites and to access those sites by clicking them in the list.

To add a site to your favorites list, follow these steps:

1. Display the Web site that you want to add to your list.
2. Open the **Favorites** menu and click the **Add to Favorites** command.
3. In the Add Favorite dialog box, shown in Figure 10.4, type a name for the page (if you're not satisfied with the default name that is provided).

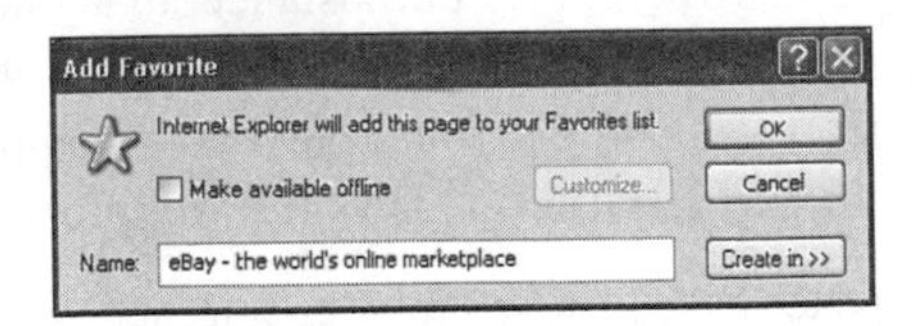


**FIGURE 10.4**
*Add favorite sites to your Favorites list.*

4. Click **OK**.

After you have added a site to your Favorites list, you can go to that site by clicking the **Favorites** button. In the Favorites bar that is displayed, click the site you want to visit.

## USING THE HISTORY LIST

If you have recently visited a site you liked, but can't remember its address, you can view the History list. From this list, you can then view the sites and pages you have visited in the last several weeks. From this list, you can find the site you want and click the link to go to that site.

Follow these steps to view and go to a site in the History list:

1. Click the **History** button. The History bar is displayed.
2. Select the week and day you want to review and the site you want to visit. Finally, click the specific page at that site. That page is displayed.
3. Click the **Close** button to close the History bar.

## SETTING YOUR HOME PAGE AND SECURITY OPTIONS

To further customize Internet Explorer, you can use the Internet Options dialog box to make other changes. In this dialog box, you can select a home page (the site that is displayed when you log on and when you click the **Home** button). You can also set security features and make more advanced changes. For instance, many home users are using a cable Internet connection. Because these types of connections are connected 24/7, it's important you protect your computer from outsiders. To do so, you can use Windows firewall protection.

Follow these steps to make changes to your Internet options:

1. Click **Tools** and then click the **Internet Options** command.
2. On the General tab, shown in Figure 10.5, you can do any of the following:

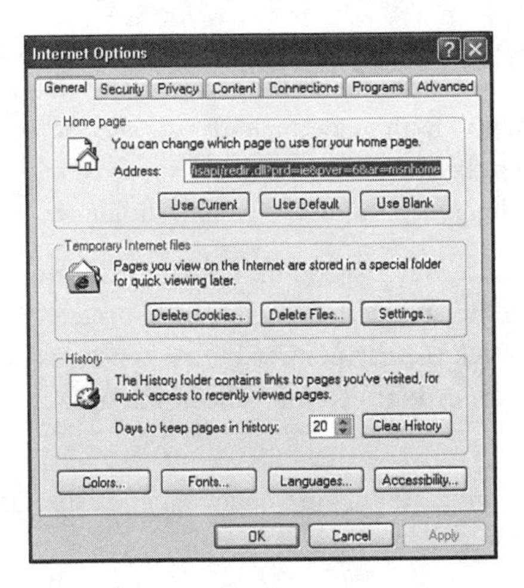


**FIGURE 10.5**

*Set basic Internet options on the General tab.*

To set a new home page, type it in the Address text box. You can also go to the page you want to use as the home page and click the **Use Current** button. To use the default home page, click the **Use Default** button.

To clear the history list, click the **Clear History** button. You might do this to keep others from browsing through a list of sites you have visited or to free up the disk space Windows XP uses to store this history list.

3. Make any other changes. The following highlights other common changes:

   To set security levels, click the **Security** tab and then select the zone to which to add sites. For instance, select **Restricted** sites. Then click the **Sites** button and type the sites that you want to restrict access to.

   To set privacy levels click the **Privacy** tab. Then drag the Privacy slider bar to select the level you want. The dialog box gives a description of each of your choices.

To enable Content Advisor (useful if children often use your Internet connection), click the **Content** tab and then click the **Enable** button in the Content Advisor section. You can then select the rating levels for different types of categories including language, nudity, sex, and violence.

To turn on firewall protection, click the **Connections** tab and then select the connection you want to protect. Click **Settings**, click the **Properties** button for the connection, and then click the **Advanced** tab. Check the firewall option to turn it on.

4. When you are done making changes, click the **OK** button to close all open dialog boxes.

## EXITING AND LOGGING OFF THE INTERNET

To exit Internet Explorer, click its **Close** button or select **File**, **Close**. When you exit Internet Explorer, you may be prompted to log off your Internet provider. Click **Yes** or **Disconnect Now**. If you are not prompted and you use a dial-up connection, be sure to log off. Right-click the connection icon in the system tray and select **Disconnect** (this does not apply to users of an always-on connection like cable or DSL).

In this lesson you learned the basics of using Internet Explorer to browse the Internet. Turn to the next lesson for information on using another one of Windows XP's communication features, the Fax Console.

# LESSON 11
# Sending and Receiving Faxes

*In this lesson you learn how to send and receive faxes with Microsoft Windows XP.*

## CONFIGURING THE FAX CONSOLE

Before you can use your fax modem to send and receive faxes, you must set it up in Windows, entering information about the fax phone number and fax device. To help you with this process, Windows XP includes the Fax Configuration Wizard. This program starts the first time you open the Fax Console. To do so, click **Start**, **All Programs**, **Accessories**, **Communications**, **Fax**, and finally **Fax Console**. Figure 11.1 shows the Fax Console window.

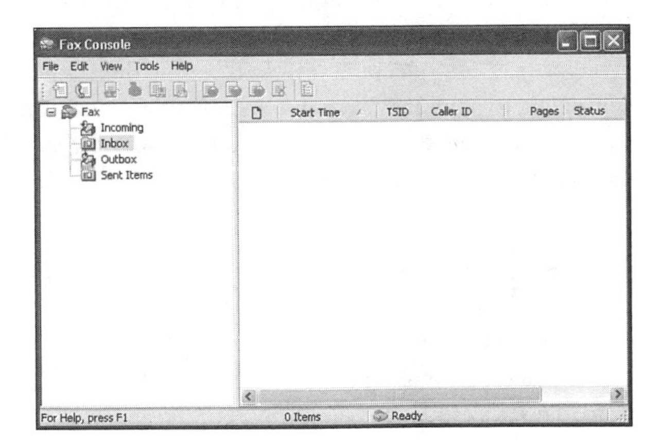


**FIGURE 11.1**
*Use the Fax Console to send and receive faxes.*

To start the Fax Configuration Wizard manually (if it does not start when you open Fax Console), click **Tools** from within Fax Console and then click the **Configure Fax** command.

To set up your fax, complete each step in the wizard, entering information and clicking **Next** to move to the next step. You can expect to complete the following:

- Enter your contact information (name, fax number, e-mail address, company, and other phone information).
- Select the fax device for sending and receiving and enter the TSID and CSID.

**TIP**

**TSID and CSID** A TSID is a line that identifies your fax when it sends a fax. You can type your business name or fax number. CSID is a text line that identifies your fax machine when it receives a fax.

- Select how received faxes are handled (printed directly to the printer or stored in a folder). If you choose to print the faxes on receipt, you can select the printer from the drop-down list. If you select to store the faxes in a folder (which you can then open and view the faxes in that folder), select this option, and then select the folder to use.

## SENDING A FAX

After the Fax Console is set up, you can use it to send and receive faxes. To help you create and send a fax, Windows XP provides a Fax Send Wizard. This wizard leads you through the steps for creating and sending a fax cover page.

To send a fax using the wizard, follow these steps:

1. If the Fax Console is not open, click **Start**, **All Programs**, **Accessories**, **Communications**, **Fax**, and finally **Fax Send Wizard**.

   If the Fax Console is open, click **File,** and then click the **Send a Fax** command. Both start the Send Fax Wizard.

2. Click **Next** to move from the welcome screen to the first step.

3. Enter the name and fax number of the recipient (see Figure 11.2). Click **Next**.

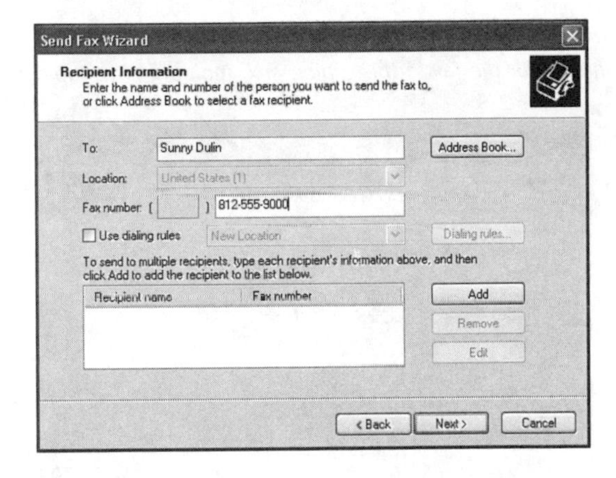


**FIGURE 11.2**
*Enter the recipient name and fax number.*

4. If you want to use a different cover page template, display the template drop-down list and select the template you want.

5. Type a subject and the note for the fax cover sheet (see Figure 11.3). Click **Next**.

6. Select when to send the fax. Your options are shown in Figure 11.4. Click **Next**.

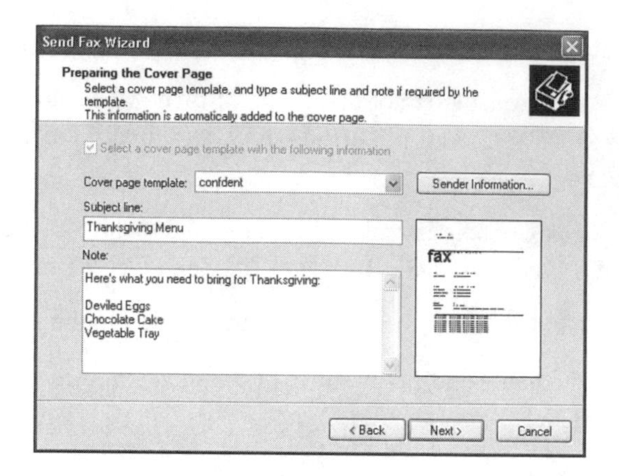


**FIGURE 11.3**

*Type the contents for the fax in this dialog box, including the subject and note.*

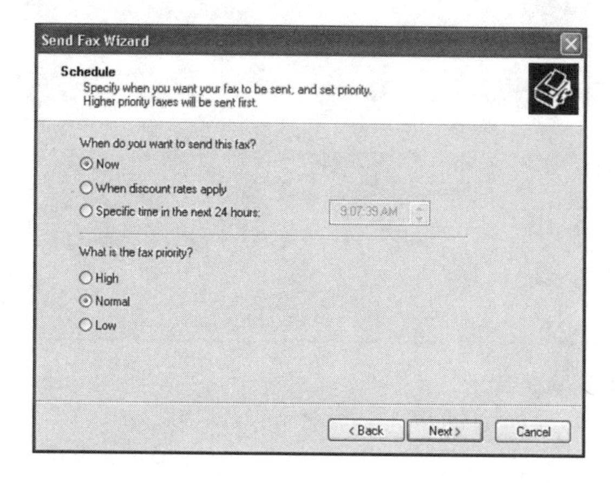


**FIGURE 11.4**

*You can send the fax immediately or schedule it for delivery at another time.*

7. Click **Finish**. The fax is sent at the time you selected for step 6.

You can also fax documents created in Windows programs by "printing" to the fax; the program will use the fax modem you have set up with the configuration wizard.

To fax a document, open the document you want to fax and then select **File**, **Print**. In the Print dialog box, select **Fax** for the printer. Complete the recipient and other information for the fax, clicking **Next** to complete each step in the fax wizard. The document is then faxed to that recipient.

## RECEIVING AND VIEWING A FAX

When you use the Fax Configuration Wizard to set up your fax modem, the modem receives any incoming faxes and handles them according to the option you selected. If you selected to print the faxes on receipt, they are printed on the printer you selected. If you selected to store them in a folder, they are placed in that folder. You can open that folder, and then view the faxes. You can also view faxes from the Fax Console by selecting **Inbox** in the Fax list. To open a fax, double-click it. You can then print from this preview window (see Figure 11.5).

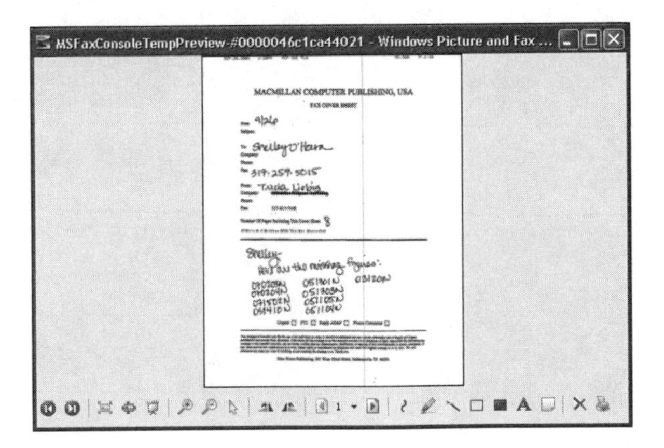


**FIGURE 11.5**
*You can open faxes in your Inbox, and then print them.*

In this lesson you learned how to use your fax modem to send and receive faxes. The next lesson starts a new topic, using a scanner or digital camera to create, print, and e-mail pictures.

**CAUTION**

**Can't Receive?** If you have problems receiving faxes, your fax device may not be set up to receive faxes. You can enable send and receive. To do so, click **Start**, **Control Panel**, **Printers and Other Hardware**, and finally, **Printers and Faxes**. Right-click the fax device, right-click **Receive**, and then click **Auto**.

# Lesson 12
# Working with Pictures

*In this lesson you learn how to work with different imaging devices, most notably scanners and digital cameras. Microsoft Windows XP includes many new features for printing, e-mailing, and ordering online prints for pictures.*

## Using a Scanner or Digital Camera

Digital cameras have become popular add-ons to the home computer. You can use these cameras to take photographs, and then copy them from the camera to your computer. When on the computer, you can edit, print, e-mail, or order online prints.

In addition, scanners are another popular add-on. With a scanner, you can take any image—photographs, drawings, documents, and so on—and scan the image, saving it as a file on your computer. Like pictures, you can then modify, print, and e-mail the image. You can even include the image within a document. For example, you can scan a picture of your family and insert it in your annual Christmas letter.

The exact steps for using your particular camera and scanner vary depending on the model you have. Therefore, you need to consult the documentation that came with the hardware to learn how to take pictures or scan images. This lesson explains how to set up a scanner and camera and tells you the types of things you can do after these images are stored on your computer.

## SETTING UP A SCANNER OR DIGITAL CAMERA

Windows XP recognizes common cameras and scanners, so often you need only attach the device to your computer and Windows XP recognizes the new hardware and sets it up automatically. You know this is happening because Windows XP alerts you with messages that pop up from the system tray.

If you have a scanner or camera that Windows XP does not recognize, you can set it up manually using the Scanner and Camera Installation Wizard. Follow these steps:

1. Click **Start**, and then click **Control Panel**.
2. Click **Printers and Other Hardware**.
3. Click the **Scanners and Cameras Control Panel** icon.
4. Double-click the **Add Device** icon to start the Scanner and Camera Installation Wizard.
5. Follow the steps in the wizard, entering or selecting the correct settings and clicking **Next** to move from one step to the next. The basic steps ask you to select the manufacturer and model of your particular device (scanner or camera). You also select the port to which the device is attached as well as enter an identifying name for the device. When you've entered all the information, click **Finish** to complete the setup.

**TIP**

**Back Up a Step** If you need to make a different selection, you can click **Back** to go back a step in the wizard.

**CAUTION**

**Driver Files** For any hardware add-on to work properly, it requires a driver file. Windows XP includes drivers for many popular printers, scanners, cameras, and other add-ons. Because not all drivers are tested with

Windows XP, you may find that Windows XP does not include a driver for your particular scanner (or other hardware). If this is the case, check the Windows XP site or the manufacturer of the scanner (or other hardware) for updated drivers.

## Printing Pictures

To organize pictures, Windows XP includes a special folder named My Pictures. You should consider placing all pictures within this folder. You can create subfolders within the main My Pictures folder to store similar pictures together.

When you open a folder that contains pictures, and then select picture files, the Task pane displays picture-related tasks. Figure 12.1 shows some pictures from a digital camera. You can print pictures on a regular printer or on a special photo printer.

**FIGURE 12.1**

*In folders with pictures, the Task pane displays picture-related tasks.*

TIP

**Photo Printers** You don't get photo-quality pictures with a regular computer printer. You can, though, purchase special photo printers and photo paper. Expect to pay from $200 to $800 or more for a special photo printer. Visit computer retail stores to see the various options. The best way to pick a printer is to check the actual printouts from various printers to find one with an acceptable print quality.

Follow these steps to print pictures:

1. Open the folder that contains the pictures you want to print.
2. Click **Print** pictures in the Task pane. This starts the Photo Printing Wizard.
3. Follow the steps in the wizard, clicking **Next** to move from step to step. You can select which pictures are printed (see Figure 12.2). You can check or uncheck individual pictures to make your selections. You can clear all selected pictures by clicking **Clear All**. Or you can select all pictures by clicking **Select All**.

   With the following steps, you select the printer to use, and then the layout for the pictures (full page, 8×10, 5×7, and other common photo sizes). When the pictures are printed, you see the final step of the wizard, telling you the pictures have been printed. Click **Finish** to close the Photo Printing Wizard.

TIP

**Include Pictures in a Document** You can also include pictures (photos or scanned images) within documents. The exact steps vary depending on the program. In Word for Windows, for example, you use the **Insert**, **Picture**, **From File** command. Check your program documentation for exact instructions on inserting pictures in your particular program(s).

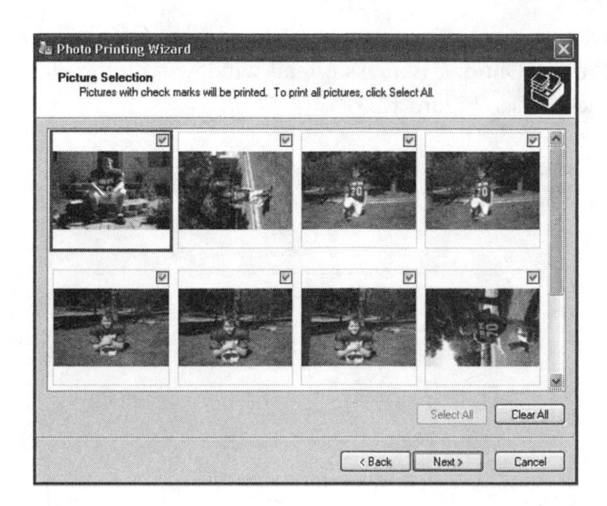


**FIGURE 12.2**
*You can check pictures you want to print and uncheck pictures you don't want to print.*

## E-MAIL PICTURES

Sharing pictures with friends and family is fun. In addition to printing, you can also e-mail pictures using the E-mail picture command in the Task pane. Follow these steps:

1. Open the folder that contains the pictures you want to e-mail.
2. Select the picture(s) you want to send. Pictures are like regular files. You can change how they are displayed using the View menu, and you can select them just like you select regular files. (See Lesson 6, "Managing Files," for help with selecting files.)

3. In the File and Folder Tasks area of the Task pane, click **E-mail this file**. You are prompted to optimize the image (which speeds sending and opening the picture).
4. Make your optimization selection and click **OK**. Windows opens an Outlook Express e-mail window with the picture attached (see Figure 12.3).

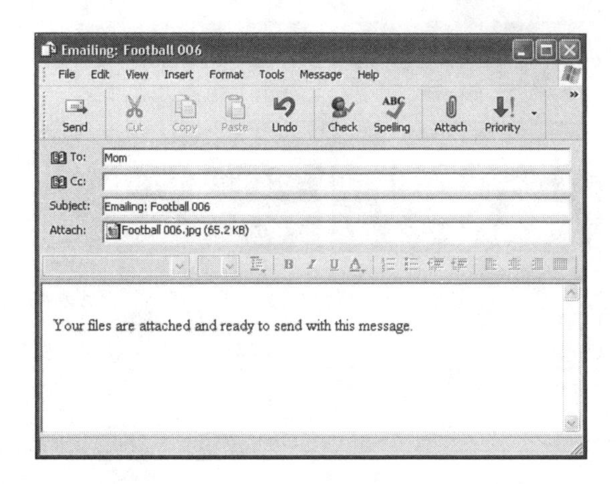


**FIGURE 12.3**
*Complete the e-mail address, type a message, and click* ***Send*** *to send the picture.*

5. Complete the e-mail address and any message you want to send with the picture attachment. Then click the **Send** button. See Lesson 9, "Sending E-mail," for more information on sending messages.

**TIP**

**Working with Picture Files** The names used for picture folders and files are not usually very descriptive (usually the date the images were taken or transferred to the computer). You can rename, delete, move, or copy these files just like any file. See Lesson 6 for more help on renaming, deleting, copying, and working with files.

## Ordering Photo Prints from the Internet

In addition to printing and e-mailing pictures, you can also select to order photoshop-quality prints from the Internet. Windows XP includes a wizard that leads you step by step through the process of ordering prints from popular print services including Kodak Online. You can get pricing information when you order the prints. Also, expect to pay a small shipping charge. For payment, you have to supply a credit card number and shipping information. Pictures usually arrive in a couple of days.

**TIP**

**Other Options** If your digital camera has a memory card, you can often take this card to a local print service and order prints from the card. Check with your favorite print shop to see what digital camera services they provide.

To order copies from the Internet, you must be connected to the Internet. If you are not connected, you are prompted to do so. When you are connected, follow these steps to order prints:

1. Open the folder that contains the pictures you want to print.
2. Click **Order prints online**.
3. Complete the steps in the wizard to order your copies, clicking **Next** to move from step to step. The steps vary depending on the service you select, but you can expect to select which pictures you want to order (much like selecting which pictures to print), the size of the pictures (costs for print size are listed), and the shipping and payment information. For the final step, click **Finish** to submit your pictures.

In this lesson you learned about using imaging devices including a scanner and digital camera. You also learned about some of the picture features of Windows XP. The next lesson covers another fun topic, music and entertainment.

# Lesson 13
# Playing Music

*In this lesson you learn about the musical features of Microsoft Windows XP including playing simple sound files with Sound Recorder as well as regular audio CDs with Media Player.*

## Playing and Recording Sounds with Sound Recorder

You can use the Sound Recorder to play back and record sounds. You can record your own sounds and insert the sound files into your documents or attach them to an e-mail. To use Sound Recorder, you need a sound card and speakers, which are standard on nearly all newer computers. To record sounds, you need a microphone attached to your sound card.

### Playing Sounds

Follow these steps to play a sound file:

1. Click **Start**, **All Programs**, **Accessories**, **Entertainment**, and select **Sound Recorder**. You see the Sound Recorder window.
2. Click **File** and then click the **Open** command.
3. Change to the drive and folder that contains the sound file you want to play. See Lesson 5, "Using My Computer to Organize Your Folders," for help on navigating among folders.

**TIP**

**Try a Sample Sound** To sample one of the Windows sounds, select the **Windows\Media** folder.

4. Double-click the sound file to open it in Sound Recorder (see Figure 13.1). Then click the **Play** button to hear the file .

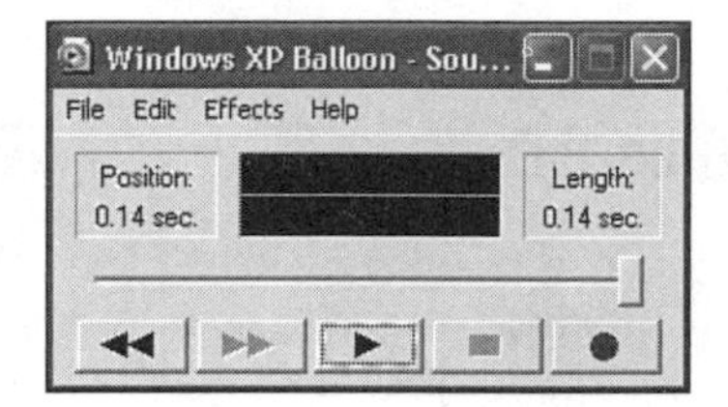


**FIGURE 13.1**
*You can play sound files in Sound Recorder.*

5. Click the **Close** button to close the Sound Recorder window.

## Recording Sounds

You can also record sounds using Sound Recorder. To do so, follow these steps:

**CAUTION**

**Attach Your Microphone** To record sounds, you must have a microphone or other sound input device connected. Check with your sound system for instructions on connecting and testing this device.

1. Start **Sound Recorder**.
2. Click **File** and then click the **New** command.

3. Click the **Record** button .
4. Speak into the microphone to record your sound. When you are done recording, click the **Stop** button .
5. To save your sound, click **File** and then click the **Save As** command. Select a folder, type a filename, and click **Save**. See Lesson 4, "Working with Documents," for more information on saving files.
6. Click the **Close** button to close the Sound Recorder window.

## PLAYING AN AUDIO CD

In addition to being able to play back sound files, you can play audio CDs using Windows Media Player. You can use this media player to listen to the background music of your choice as you work. Note that the quality of the playback is determined by the quality of your speakers and the quality of the source audio format. Unless you've invested in high-quality PC speakers, don't expect home stereo quality!

To play an audio CD, simply insert it into your CD drive. Windows Media Player should automatically begin to play the CD (see Figure 13.2). If the CD does not play (your drive may not be set up for Autoplay), click **Start**, **All Programs**, **Accessories**, **Entertainment**, and finally, **Windows Media Player**. Then click the **Play** button.

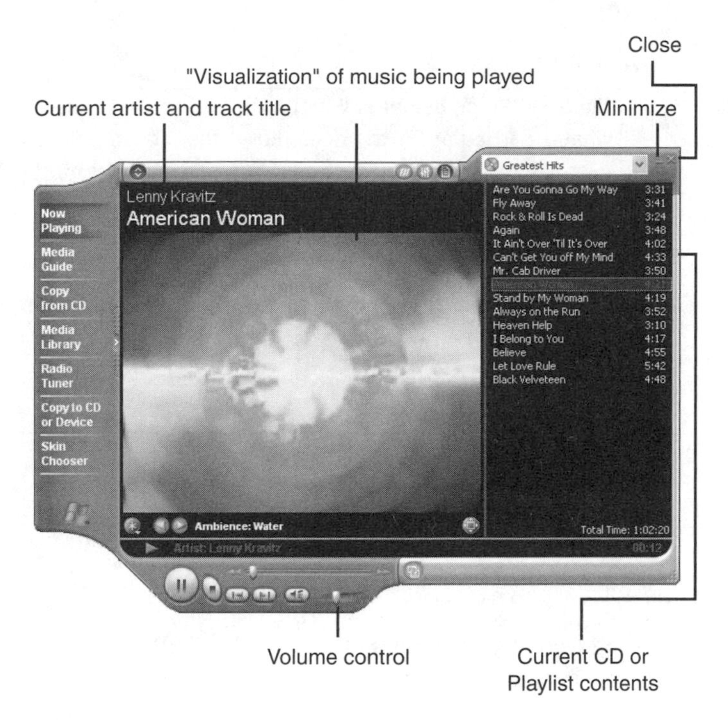


**FIGURE 13.2**

*You can use the controls in the Windows Media Player window to play a different track, display a different visualization, and make other changes.*

## WORKING WITH WINDOWS MEDIA PLAYER

The Media Player window provides several buttons for controlling the playback of music and other audio. You can do any of the following:

- To play a different track, double-click it in the track list. Or to play the next track, click **Next**. To play the previous track, click **Previous** .

TIP

**Not Sure Which Button Is Which?** If you are not sure what a particular button does, hover the mouse pointer over it for two or three seconds. The name of the button pops up.

- To change the volume, drag the volume control.
- To display a different visualization, click **Next visualization** or **Previous visualization**.

PLAIN ENGLISH

**Visualization** A visualization is a moving graphic that visually represents an interpretation of the music.

- To stop the playback, click **Stop**.
- To keep the music playing, but hide the Media Player window, click its **Minimize** button.
- To stop the music and close Media Player, click the **Close** button.

## USING OTHER WINDOWS MEDIA PLAYER FEATURES

In addition to simple playback, you can also use Windows Media Player for several other music tasks. You can do any of the following:

- You can copy tracks from a CD to your computer. You can then play back the song from the computer rather than the audio CD. You can also copy the song track from your computer to a CD disk if you have a recordable CD drive or to a portable music player such as an MP3 player. Use the **Copy from CD** and **Copy to CD or Device** buttons in the Media Player window for these features.

**PLAIN ENGLISH**

**MP3** MP3 is a popular file format for music files. You can find MP3 files on various Internet sites. With an MP3 player, you can copy tunes to your player and take the music with you, much like a Sony Walkman. In addition to MP3 files, you can find other standard music file types.

**PLAIN ENGLISH**

**WMA** WMA is another popular music file format that is the preferred format for Windows XP playback devices.

**CAUTION**

**Copy Protection** When copying audio files, be sure you understand the legal ramifications of copyright protection. Recently there's been a big brouhaha over certain sites such as Napster that provided free music. While that site is still in existence, you can no longer get free music from the site. You can find other free sites as well as music sites that enable you to purchase songs.

- You can tune into your favorite radio station, listening to taped or live radio broadcasts right from your computer. You can select from several preset radio stations, including BBC World, NPR (National Public Radio), Billboard, and others. To use this feature, you must be connected to the Internet. Use the **Radio Tuner** button in the Media Player window to find and list to radio stations (see Figure 13.3).
- Use the Media Library to access all the audio, video, and radio stations set up on your computer. You can set up playlists on this page as well as organize contents by category. For example, you can arrange music files by album, artist, or genre.

- You can change the appearance of the Media Player window, choosing a different skin. To do so, click the **Skin Chooser** button and then select from various skins.

TIP

**Skin** A **skin** is a layer over an application that changes how it looks.

**FIGURE 13.3**
*Tune into the radio tuner from the Radio Tuner tab in Windows Media Player.*

TIP

**More Information?** For more information on any of these features, consult the online help for Windows Media Player. Click **Start**, **Help and Support**, and then click **Music, video, games, and photos** in the Pick a Help topic list. On the next help screen, click **Music and sounds**. You see the topics within this category. Click **Using Windows Media Player** and then click any of the available topics for detailed help information.

- Use the Media Guide to access **`WindowsMedia.com`**, an online media site where you can get information about music, radio, movies, and other topics (see Figure 13.4). You must be connected to the Internet to access this online guide.

In this lesson you learned about the various sound and music features of Windows XP. Turn to the next lesson for help on some of the other accessory programs included with Windows XP.

**FIGURE 13.4**
*Use the Media Guide to get entertainment news.*

# LESSON 14

# Using Other Windows XP Accessories

*In this lesson you learn about some of the accessory programs included in Microsoft Windows XP. You can find these mini-applications within the Accessories menu.*

## USING WINDOWS MOVIE MAKER

One of the hot features with computers is making movies, and Windows XP includes an updated version of the Windows Movie Maker program first included in Windows Me. You can use this accessory program to view and edit movies. To create your own movies, you need a camera capable of recording digital videos. You can then download the video from your camera to your computer and use Windows Movie Maker to view and edit it. You can also import other videos or music to use in Windows Movie Maker. Figure 14.1 shows one of Windows sample movie files displayed in Windows Movie Maker.

TIP

**Get Help** For detailed information on all the features of Windows Movie Maker and any accessory program, use commands in the program's Help menu.

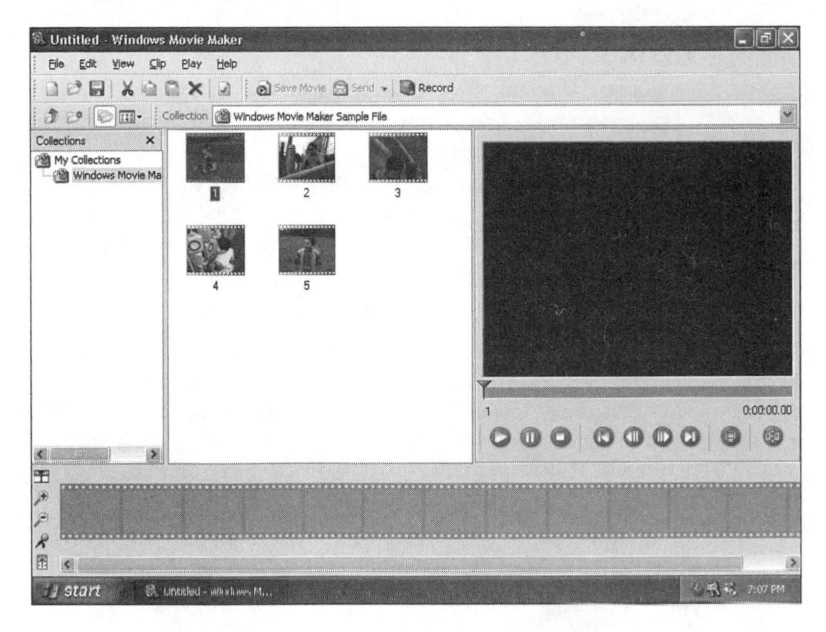


**FIGURE 14.1**

*You can create, edit, and play back movie files with Windows Movie Maker.*

## PLAYING GAMES

Windows provides several games that you can play to break up your workday with a little entertainment. Playing games is also a good way to help you get the hang of using the mouse if you are a beginner. For example, playing Solitaire can help you practice clicking and dragging. You can find the games by clicking **Start**, **All Programs**, and then **Games**. Figure 14.2 shows Solitaire.

**CAUTION**

**Games Not Installed?** Depending on the type of installation you performed, some features may not be installed. You can add them as needed. To do so, click **Start, Control Panel**. Click the **Add or Remove Programs** category, and then click the **Add/Remove Windows Components** button in the Add or Remove Programs window. Check the features to install and then click **Next**. Windows then adds and configures the additional components. This procedure works for games as well as other options such as fax features, system tools, desktop themes, and other Windows components.

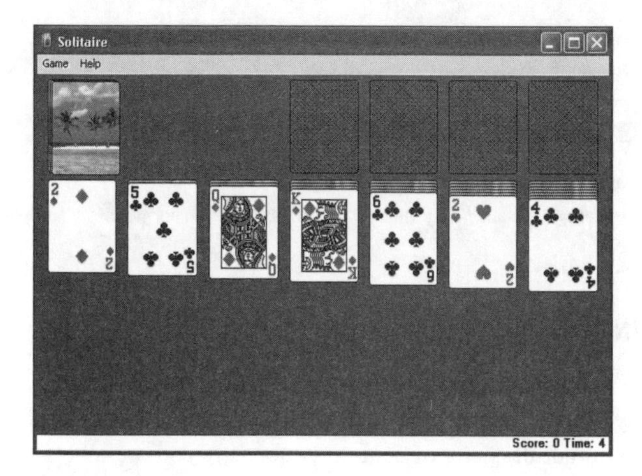


**FIGURE 14.2**
*You can play one of many games, including the popular Solitaire.*

## USING CALCULATOR

One of my favorite accessory programs is the Calculator. It's easy to pop it open and perform calculations. You can type equations on the Numeric keypad (make sure Num Lock is enabled) or click the buttons on the calculator. You can add, subtract, multiply, divide, figure percentages, and more with this handy tool shown in Figure 14.3.

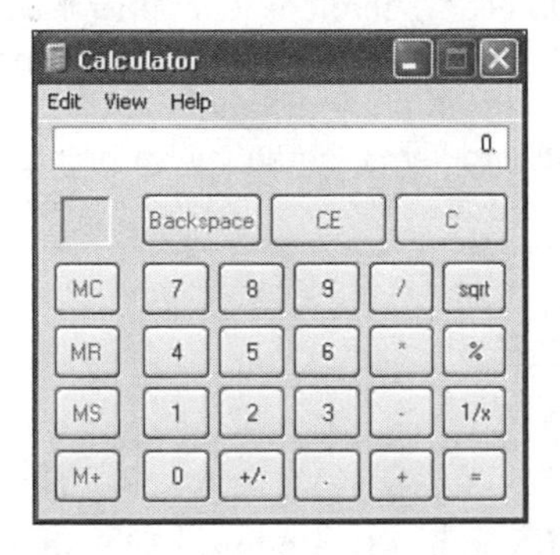


**FIGURE 14.3**
*Use Calculator to perform basic calculations.*

TIP

**More Features** For a more complex scientific calculator, start **Calculator** and then click **View**, **Scientific**. You then have available more sophisticated calculation features.

## Using the Command Prompt

If you are a longtime computer user, you probably are familiar with the old DOS prompt. There may be times when you want to access the DOS prompt from Windows XP. For example, you might want to run a DOS application or use DOS commands. Alternatively, you might have programs (especially games) that run in DOS. You can run any program by typing the appropriate DOS command. Windows XP provides a Command Prompt window that you can open while working in Windows.

Like other accessory programs, start the Command Prompt by clicking **Start**, **All Programs**, **Accessories**, **Command Prompt**.

Type the desired command and press **Enter**. To close the Command Prompt window, click its **Close** button or type `EXIT` and press **Enter**.

**CAUTION**

**Running DOS Programs** Windows XP does not contain any DOS code; therefore, support for DOS applications is limited. While many DOS applications will run, they may not install properly, and you can expect other compatibility problems, notably with programs that use sound cards.

## USING WORDPAD

WordPad is a simple word processing program with basic features for typing, editing, and formatting text. If you create simple documents, WordPad might suit you just fine. Figure 14.4 shows the WordPad window. To enter text, just start typing. To make formatting changes, use the toolbar buttons or the commands in the Format menu. To make editing changes, use the commands in the Edit menu.

If you want to save your document, use the **File**, **Save As** command. For more information on saving a file, see Lesson 4, "Working with Documents."

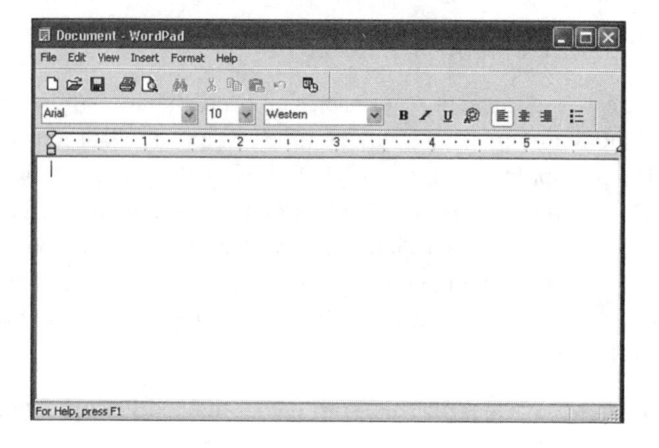


**FIGURE 14.4**
*WordPad is a simple word processing program included with Windows XP.*

TIP

**Editing Text Files** Another program for editing or viewing simple text (.txt) files is Notepad. You can start this program by clicking **Start**, **All Programs**, **Accessories**, **Notepad**. It has even fewer features than WordPad, but it is useful for viewing README files commonly included with programs.

## USING PAINT

You can use Paint to create simple drawings. You can draw lines and shapes, add text, and change the colors. If you make a mistake, use the Eraser to erase part of the drawing.

To start paint, click **Start**, **All Programs**, **Accessories**, and choose **Paint**. Figure 14.5 shows the Paint window.

**FIGURE 14.5**
*You can create simple diagrams and drawings using Paint.*

In paint, you can do any of the following:

- To draw a shape, click the tool in the toolbar. Then click and drag within the drawing area to draw the shape.
- To add color, you can use the **Fill With Color** tool or the **Airbrush** tool.
- To draw a text box, use the **Text** tool to drag the text box. Then type the text to include. You can change the font, font size, and font style (bold, italic, or underline).
- If you make a mistake and want to get rid of something you have added, you can use the **Eraser** tool. Click the **Eraser** tool. Click the size you want the eraser to be. Move the pointer to the drawing area. Hold down the mouse button, and drag across the part you want to erase.
- If you want to save your drawing, use the **File**, **Save As** command. For more information on saving a file, see Lesson 4.

TIP

**Select Colors** Use the color box (at the bottom of the Paint window) to select colors for the lines and fills of the objects you draw. Click the color you want to use for the border. For filled objects, right-click the color you want to use as the fill color.

The best way to learn any of the accessory programs, including Paint is to experiment. Also, use the Help menu within the program to look up help topics.

In this lesson you learned about some of the most commonly used accessory programs. You can also try out others listed on the Accessories menus. The next lesson covers some of the changes you can make to personalize Windows XP.

# Lesson 15

# Customizing the Windows XP Desktop

*In this lesson you learn how you can change the look of the Microsoft Windows XP taskbar, Start menu, and desktop to suit your own personal style.*

## Customizing the Taskbar

Windows XP enables you to customize the taskbar and system tray (also called the notification area). To make any changes, display the Taskbar and Start Menu Properties dialog box by following these steps:

1. Right-click a blank part of the taskbar and select the **Properties** command from the pop-up menu. You see the Taskbar and Start Menu Properties dialog (see Figure 15.1).
2. Make any changes. You can unlock the taskbar so that you can move it around. You can hide the taskbar so that you have more desktop room. You can always redisplay the taskbar by pointing to the bottom of the desktop. You can also select to hide the clock, hide inactive icons, and make other changes.

TIP

**Not Sure About an Option?** If you aren't sure what an option does, right-click it and then select **What's This** to display a pop-up explanation.

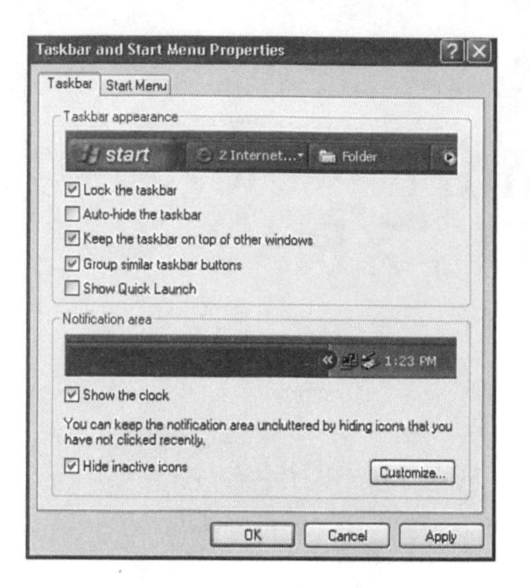


**FIGURE 15.1**

*Use this dialog box to customize the taskbar and system tray (also called the notification area).*

3. When you are done making changes, click the **OK** button.

**TIP**

**Move and Resize** You can also move the taskbar to another location on the desktop and change its size. To move the taskbar, put the mouse pointer on a blank part of the taskbar and drag it to the location you want. To resize the taskbar, put the mouse pointer on the border and drag to resize.

## Customizing the Start Menu

In addition to changing the taskbar, you can also change how the Start menu looks. For example, you may prefer the Classic Start menu (one from previous Windows versions) or you may prefer to list more or fewer programs on the left pane. You can also select whether to list the Internet and e-mail programs as well as select which programs are used for these commands.

Follow these steps to make changes:

1. Right-click a blank part of the taskbar and select **Properties** from the pop-up menu.
2. Click the **Start Menu** tab.
3. From this tab, click **Classic Start menu** if you prefer that menu style.
4. To customize the Windows XP Start menu, click the **Customize** button next to this option. You see the Customize Start Menu dialog box shown in Figure 15.2.

**FIGURE 15.2**
*You can select the style of the icons, the number of programs listed, as well as whether Internet and e-mail programs are included.*

5. Do any of the following:

   Select to display large or small icons.

   Select the number of recently used programs to list on the left side of the Start menu.

   To turn off the commands for starting your Internet or e-mail program, uncheck the option(s). To use a different program for either, display the drop-down list next to the program type, and then select the program to use.

6. Click **OK** to put your changes into effect.

TIP

**More Advanced Options** For more advanced options, click the **Advanced** tab in the Customize Start Menu dialog box, and then make any changes.

## CUSTOMIZING THE DESKTOP

You have lots of choices for customizing the desktop. You can use a desktop theme, change the color scheme, use a screen saver, and more. All of these options are available in the Display Properties dialog box.

PLAIN ENGLISH

**Desktop Theme** Desktop themes consist of a background, sounds, icons, and other elements. Windows XP offers numerous color-coordinated themes to choose from or you can create your own.

To make any of these changes, right-click an empty spot on your desktop, and select **Properties** from the pop-up menu that appears. The Display Properties dialog box appears, with the Themes tab displayed. The following sections describe the most common changes. You can pick and choose which you'd like to try.

To make one change, select the options and click **OK** to close the dialog box. To make several changes, select the option and then click **Apply**, leaving the dialog box open to make additional changes. When you are done customizing the display, click **OK**.

## Using a Desktop Theme

To use a desktop theme, display the **Themes** drop-down list, and select a theme. The theme you selected is previewed in the Sample window. Figure 15.3 shows the Windows Classic theme.

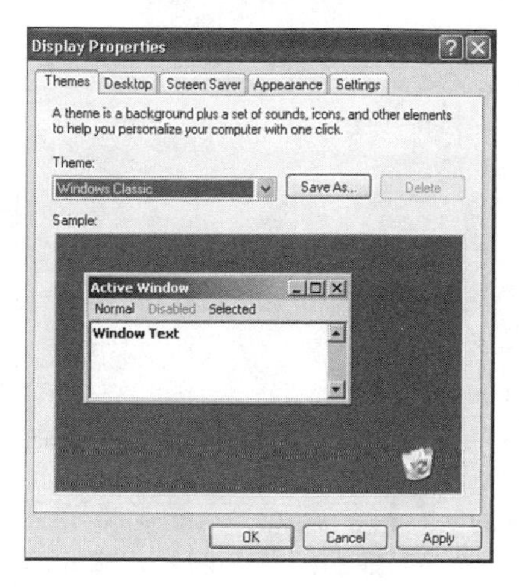


**FIGURE 15.3**
*You can apply a set of options, called a theme.*

TIP

**Locating Additional Themes** If the theme you want to use does not appear in the Themes drop-down list, select either **More Themes** or **Browse** from the list. Selecting **More Themes** opens a Web site offering themes; selecting **Browse** enables you to locate additional themes you may have saved to your hard drive.

## Using a Background Image

To apply a background picture or pattern to your desktop, click the **Desktop** tab. Then select the background you want to use. Figure 15.4 shows a sample background selected (Purple flower).

**FIGURE 15.4**
*Use a background image to jazz up your desktop.*

TIP

**Display Your Own Image** If you'd rather display one of your own digital pictures, click the **Browse** button on the Desktop tab. In the Browse dialog box, navigate to the folder that contains the picture, select it, and then click **Open**. For more information on navigating through folders, see Lesson 5, "Using My Computer to Organize Your Folders." The image is added to the list of Background choices; select it to use it as your background.

## USING A SCREEN SAVER

To use a screen saver, click the **Screen Saver** tab. Then display the Screen Saver drop-down list and select the image you want to use. Set the time limit using the Wait spin boxes (see Figure 15.5). When your computer is idle for the time limit you selected, the screen saver image will be displayed. You can turn off the screen saver by moving the mouse or pressing a key.

**FIGURE 15.5**
*Select a moving image to use as your screen saver.*

**TIP**

**Screen Saver Necessary?** Not really. On older monitors an image could be burned into the monitor if the same text or image was displayed for long periods of time. This is not a problem with current monitors. Screen savers are now mostly used for fun and a little bit of privacy. Also, keep in mind they do use additional RAM and system resources that could have some impact your computer's performance.

## Changing the Color Scheme

Windows XP enables you to change the sets of colors used for certain onscreen elements such as the title bar, background, and so on. These sets of colors are called *schemes*, and you can select colors that work best for you and your monitor. Lighter colors might, for example, make working in some Windows applications easier on your eyes. On the other hand, you might prefer bright and lively colors.

**PLAIN ENGLISH**

**Scheme** A scheme is a set of options, such as colors and fonts for all Windows elements. You can also use sound schemes, sets of sounds for various system events.

To make a change, click the **Appearance** tab. Display the Color Scheme drop-down list and select the scheme you want to apply. The scheme you selected is previewed in the Sample window (see Figure 15.6).

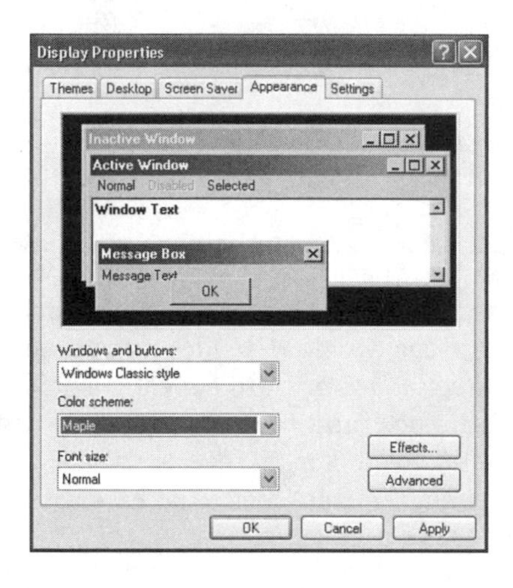


**FIGURE 15.6**
*It may be hard to see the color difference in this black-and-white figure, but the figure shows the Maple color scheme.*

## SETTING RESOLUTION AND COLOR SETTINGS

Many monitors enable you to select certain options about how they work, such as the number of colors they display or their resolution.

**PLAIN ENGLISH**

**Resolution** Resolution is a measurement of the number of pixels or picture elements displayed. An example of a common resolution is 800×600 or 1024×768.

To make a change, click the **Settings** tab. To change the resolution, drag the Screen resolution bar to the desired setting. To change the number of colors used for the display, click the **Colors** drop-down list and choose the number you want. Windows XP does not enable you to select a resolution or color depth that your computer does not support, so feel free to experiment with these options.

**TIP**

**Troubleshoot** If you are having problems with your monitor, you can start the Troubleshooter. From the Settings tab, click the **Troubleshoot** button, which starts the Video Display Troubleshooter. You can select from several different display problems, and Windows XP Troubleshooter suggests possible remedies.

Windows XP offers many other customization features, including customizing the mouse and keyboard. This lesson highlighted the most common, however. The next lesson explains how to set up programs on your computer.

# Lesson 16
# Setting Up Programs

*In this lesson you learn how to install new programs, get rid of programs you don't need, and add programs to the opening Start menu.*

## Installing Programs

When you bought your computer, it might have come with certain programs already installed. If you want to add to these, you can purchase additional programs and then install them on your system. Different programs employ different installation processes. That is, the steps vary from one program to another. Microsoft Windows XP's Add or Remove Programs feature enables you to start the installation from a CD-ROM or floppy disk. You can then follow the steps for your program.

Follow these steps to install a new program:

1. Click the **Start** button, and then click **Control Panel**.
2. Click **Add or Remove Programs**. You see the Add or Remove Programs window (see Figure 16.1).
3. Click the **Add New Programs** button.
4. Click the **CD or Floppy** button.
5. Insert the program's CD-ROM or floppy disk and click the **Next** button. Windows XP checks the floppy disk, and then the CD disk for installation programs. It then automatically selects the appropriate file, which is listed in the Run Installation Program dialog box (see Figure 16.2).

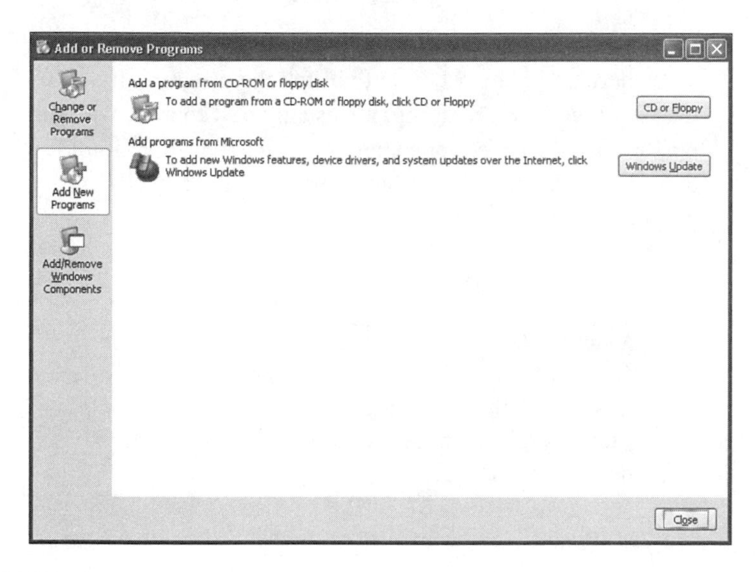


**FIGURE 16.1**

*Use this Control Panel feature to change or remove programs, install new programs, or add or remove Windows components.*

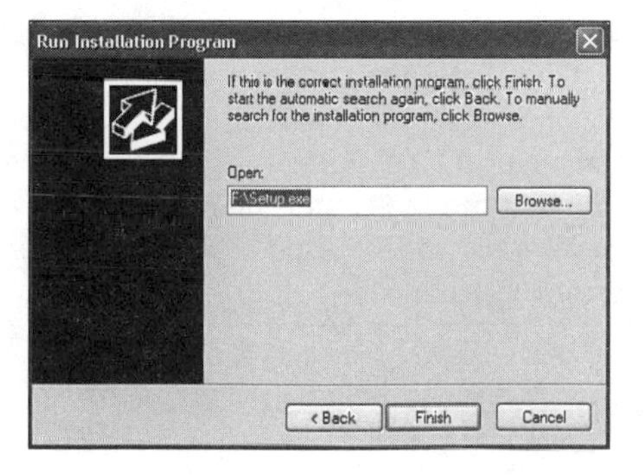


**FIGURE 16.2**

*Click Finish to run the appropriate installation file usually named Install or Setup.*

6. Click **Finish**. What happens next depends the software you are installing; follow the onscreen directions. Usually you are

asked for an installation type (partial, full, custom, and so on) and where on your hard drive to install the program. If you're unsure of what you're doing, it's usually best to stick with the default installation options a program offers. The program is then installed, and the installation program usually adds program icons to the Start menu.

**Automatic Install** Most newer programs feature an Autorun feature. Once you insert the CD into the drive, it launches the installer program automatically (unless your drive does not support Autorun or this feature has been turned off).

**Use the Run Command** If this procedure does not work, you can use the Run command to run the installation program. Insert the CD-ROM or disk into the appropriate drive, and then click the **Start** button and click the **Run** command. Enter the path and program name to run the installation program, and click **OK**. (If you don't know the name of the program or its path, click the **Browse** button and use the Browse dialog box to find the file. Look for a file called Setup or Install.) Follow the onscreen instructions.

## INSTALLING WINDOWS UPDATES

From the Add or Remove Programs dialog box, you can also connect to Microsoft's online Windows upgrade site and download any new program features. Periodically, Microsoft adds updates to Windows, including patches for any bugs (errors) in the program.

TIP

**Bug and Patch** A bug is a problem in the software code that causes problems. A patch is a small chunk of programming code that repairs the bug.

You can click the **Windows Update** button to check for any new features. You can then select to download and install them. You can also select the Windows Update command from the Start menu, under All Programs.

## Installing Windows Components

In addition to Windows update, you may also need to add or remove Windows components. Depending on the type of installation you performed, you may not have installed certain features (such as fax features). Or to save disk space, you may want to remove components you don't use.

To make a change to Windows components, follow these steps:

1. Click the **Start** button, and then click **Control Panel**.
2. Click **Add or Remove Programs**. You see the Add or Remove Programs window (see Figure 16.1).
3. Click the **Add/Remove Windows Components** button. You see the Windows Components Wizard (see Figure 16.3). Items that are checked are installed. You can uncheck items to remove them from your setup. You can also check any item to add it to your setup.
4. Check or uncheck components and then click **Next**. Insert your Windows disk if prompted. Windows configures and sets up any new components and removes any components you targeted for removal. Click **Finish** to complete the wizard.

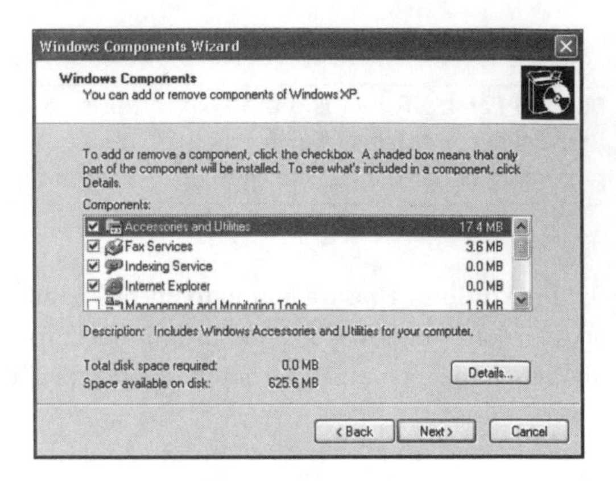


**FIGURE 16.3**
*Select which components to add or remove.*

## UNINSTALLING PROGRAMS

If you don't use a program, you can remove it from your system. Doing so can free up disk space. You could simply delete the program file(s), but these files are not always stored in one location. A program installation may store files in other places on your hard drive. Instead, uninstall the program using the Add or Remove Programs Control Panel. This removes the program and all its related files and folders from your hard disk.

**CAUTION**

**Check for Document Files** If you have any folders that contain your documents within the program folders, be sure to move them to another folder or drive so that they are not deleted with the program.

Follow these steps to uninstall a program:

1. Click the **Start** button, and then click **Control Panel**.
2. Click **Add or Remove Programs**. You see the Add or Remove Programs window (see Figure 16.1).

3. Click the **Change or Remove Programs** button.

4. Select the program you want to remove (see Figure 16.4). Then click the **Remove** button. Windows XP then removes the program. The steps vary from program to program. Simply follow the onscreen instructions.

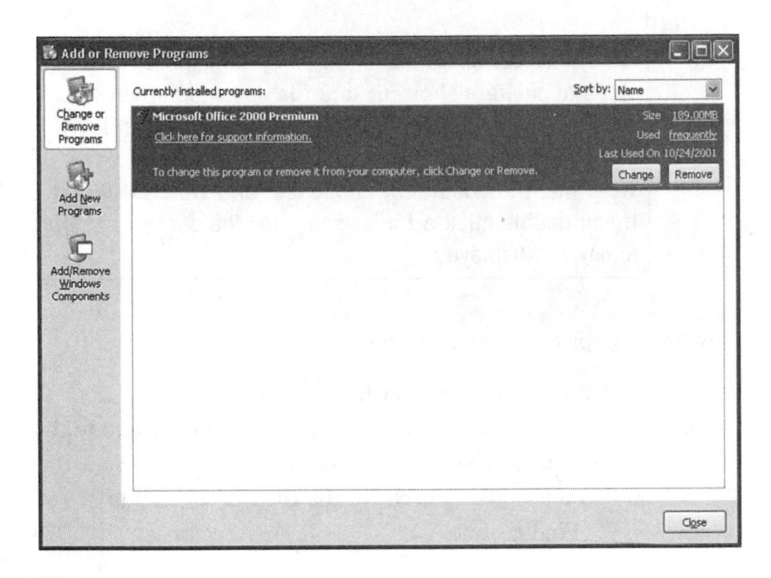


**FIGURE 16.4**
*You can get information about how often a program is used as well as remove it from this Control Panel page.*

**TIP**

**Uninstall Programs** You can purchase programs to keep track of what programs you have installed, where they are, and what changes they have made to your system. You can use such a program to uninstall programs not listed in the Windows Add or Remove Programs Control Panel.

## CREATING A SHORTCUT TO A PROGRAM

You can create shortcuts and place them on the desktop to provide quick access to programs. You can then double-click a program shortcut to quickly start that program.

TIP

**File and Folder Shortcuts** You can follow these same steps to create a shortcut to a file or folder. When you double-click a file shortcut, that file is opened in the associated program. For example, if you double-click a Word file, the document is opened, and Word is started. If you double-click a folder shortcut, the contents of that folder are displayed.

Follow these steps to create a shortcut:

1. Display the program file for which you want to create a shortcut. For help on navigating among your drives and folders, see Lesson 5, "Using My Computer to Organize Your Folders." You can also search for the file (as covered in Lesson 7, "Finding Files").
2. Right-click the file and then click the **Send To** command. From the submenu, click the **Desktop (create shortcut)** command (see Figure 16.5). Windows adds the shortcut to your desktop.

TIP

**Rename the Shortcut** Windows XP uses the program file name for the shortcut name. You can change this name to a more descriptive one. To do so, right-click the shortcut, select **Rename**, type a new name, and press **Enter**.

If your desktop becomes too cluttered with shortcut icons, you can delete them. To do so, right-click the shortcut icon and then click the

**Delete** command. Click **Yes** to delete the shortcut. Deleting a shortcut does not delete that program from your hard drive. To delete the program, you must uninstall it. See the section "Uninstalling Programs" earlier in this lesson.

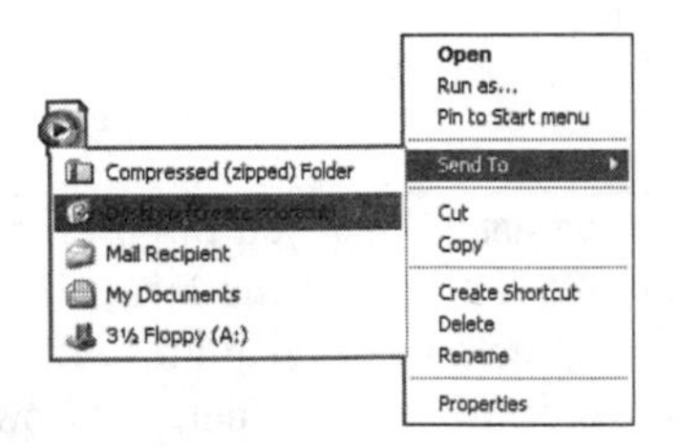


**FIGURE 16.5**
*Use the shortcut menu to create a shortcut icon to a program file.*

**TIP**

**Clean Up Your Desktop** Windows XP includes a feature for automatically removing unused desktop icons. To access this feature, right-click a blank part of the desktop and choose Properties. Click the **Desktop** tab and then click the **Customize Desktop** button. Click the **Clean Desktop Now** button to start the Desktop Cleanup Wizard. Follow the steps in the wizard to view and confirm the removal of any unused desktop icons.

## Pinning a Program to the Start Menu

When you install most programs, they are added automatically to the Start menu. If a program is not added during installation, you can add it yourself. Windows XP enables you to "pin" a program to your Start menu.

Follow these steps:

1. Display the program file for which you want to create a shortcut. For help on navigating among your drives and folders, see Lesson 5. You can also search for the file (see

Lesson 7). If the program is listed on the Start menu, you can simply display the program list.

2. Right-click the program icon and click the **Pin to Start menu** command (see Figure 16.5). The program is added to your Start menu.

TIP

**Move the Program** When you pin a program to your Start menu, it is placed in the left pane of the menu. You can drag the pinned program to the My Documents, My Pictures, or My Music folder, but nowhere else within the Start menu.

In this lesson you learned how to install and uninstall programs. You also learned how to provide quicker access to programs, creating shortcut icons or pinning a program to the Start menu. The next lesson covers troubleshooting and maintenance topics.

# LESSON 17

# Maintaining Your PC

*In this lesson you learn how to perform maintenance tasks (to avoid problems) as well as how to troubleshoot problems.*

## RESTARTING AND SHUTTING DOWN THE COMPUTER

If your computer gets stuck, one of the first things to try is restarting the computer. You may also need to restart if you make system changes; restarting puts the changes into effect.

Also, to avoid problems, you need to shut down properly before you turn off your computer. Doing so enables Microsoft Windows XP to perform behind-the-scenes tasks before shutting down.

To restart or shut down, follow these steps:

1. Click the **Start** button.
2. Click the **Turn off computer** button.
3. Select **Restart** to restart the computer, or select **Turn Off** to turn off the computer. If you selected to restart, the computer is restarted. If you selected to turn off, the computer is shut down and powers itself off. (Some older PCs may display a screen that tells you it's ready to be turned off; you must then turn off the power manually.)

TIP

**Hibernate** To hibernate the computer to conserve power, select the **Hibernate** button. Everything in computer memory is saved to the hard disk. When you "wake up" from hibernation, all programs and documents that were open are restored. This is most commonly used for laptops as it does slow down your PC's ability to shut down and boot up again.

## GETTING HELP

You can use the Windows **Help** command to get help on common topics. You can select from a list of topics, including starting Troubleshooters that help you pinpoint problems and offer suggested fixes.

Follow these steps to get help:

1. Click the **Start** button.
2. Click **Help and Support**. You see the Help and Support Center window (see Figure 17.1).
3. Click the topic you want help on. Select **Fixing a problem**, for example. You see the related topics.
4. Click the subtopic you want. The right pane lists relevant help topics. Figure 17.2 shows the topics for Printing problems.
5. Click the topic you want. When you are done reviewing the help information, click the help window's **Close** button.

**TIP**

**Search for Help** As an alternative to browsing the contents, you can search for help. Type the topic in the Search box and press **Enter**. The matching topics are listed in the Search Results pane on the left. You can click any of the matches in this pane to display the relevant help topic in the pane on the right.

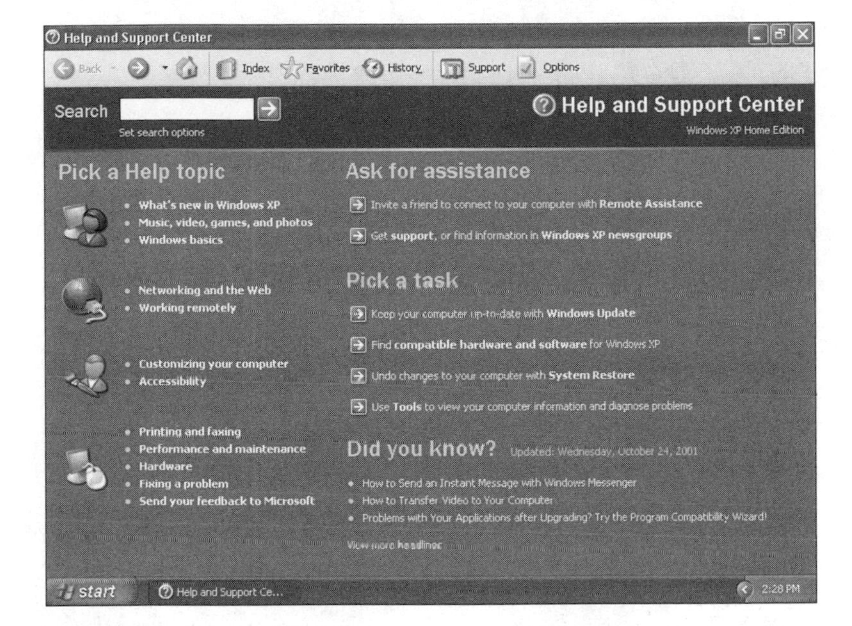


**FIGURE 17.1**
*You can get extensive help from the Windows XP help guide as well as online sources.*

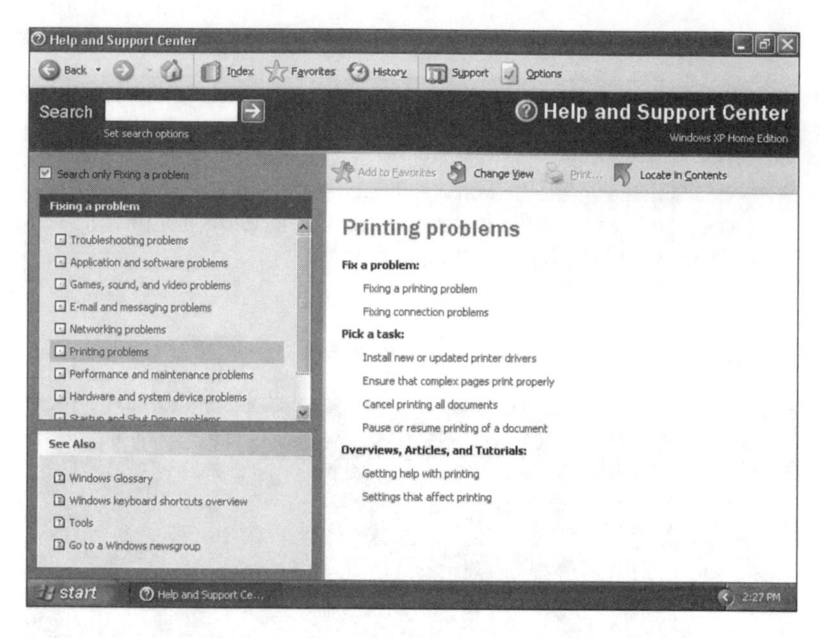


**FIGURE 17.2**
*Use Windows help to get detailed information about features as well as troubleshooting advice.*

## DISPLAYING SYSTEM PROPERTIES

When you are troubleshooting, you sometimes need to display information about your system. One place to start is with your system properties. Here you can access the Add Hardware Wizard, display the Device Manager, and more. To display system properties, open your Start menu, right-click **My Computer** and then click the **Properties** command. You can then click any of the available tabs. Figure 17.3 shows the Hardware tab of the System Properties dialog box.

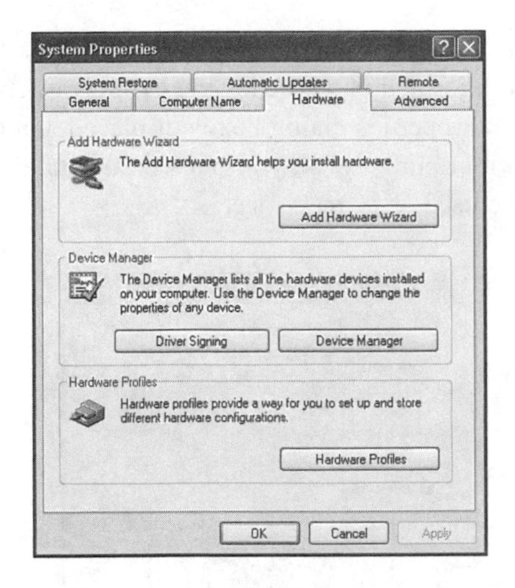


**FIGURE 17.3**
*Get information about your system from the System Properties dialog box.*

**TIP**

**More Technical Information** For more technical information including information about hardware configurations, computer components, and software, display System Information. To do so, click **Start**, **All Programs**, **Accessories**, **System Tools**, **System Information**. Click any of the listed categories to view related information.

## Displaying Disk Information

You can display information about your disks, such as the size, the amount of occupied space, and the amount of free space. You can also access system tools from this window.

Follow these steps to display disk information:

1. Open the **My Computer** icon. You can click **Start**, **My Computer**. Or if you have added the My Computer icon to your desktop, you can double-click it.

2. In the My Computer window, right-click the disk for which you want information, and click the **Properties** command. The disk's Properties dialog box is displayed. On the General tab, shown in Figure 17.4, you can see the total disk space, disk space used, and free space.

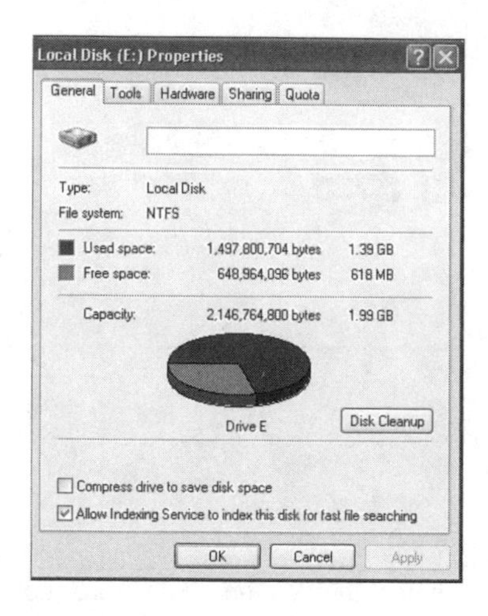


**FIGURE 17.4**
*You can view disk information from this dialog box.*

3. Click the **OK** button to close the dialog box.

## USING DISK TOOLS

In the Local Disk Properties dialog box shown in Figure 17.4, notice the Tools tab. You can click this tab to view tools for working with your hard disk. You can, for example, check a disk for errors and defragment a disk using this tab.

### CHECKING A DISK FOR ERRORS

Sometimes parts of your hard disk get damaged, and you might see an error message when you try to open or save a file. You can scan the disk for damage and fix any problems. To check for errors, click the **Check Now** button on the Tools tab (see Figure 17.5). You can select whether errors are automatically fixed and whether the scan checks and repairs bad sectors. Click **Start** to start the check.

If Check Disk finds an error, a dialog box appears explaining the error. Read the error message and choose the option you want to perform. Click **OK** to continue. Do this for each message.

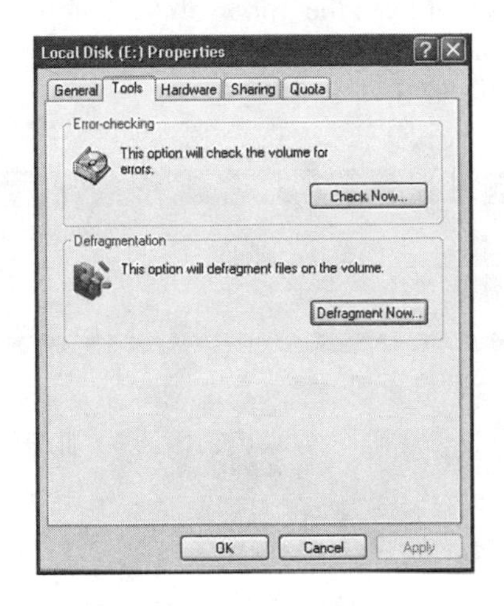


**FIGURE 17.5**
*Check a disk for errors or defragment a disk using the buttons on this tab.*

**TIP**

**Scanning After Rebooting** If you don't properly shut down Windows, Check Disk runs automatically when you restart.

## DEFRAGMENTING A DISK

When a stored on your hard drive, Windows places as much of the file as possible in the first available section (called a *cluster*), and then goes to the next cluster to put the next part of the file. Initially, this storage does not cause performance problems, but over time, your disk files become fragmented; you might find that it takes a long time to open a file or start a program. To speed access to files and to help prevent potential problems with fragmented files, you can use Disk Defragmenter to *defragment* your disk, putting files in clusters as close to each other as possible. Defragmenting your disk is a general maintenance job that you should perform every few months for best results.

You can start this tool from the Tools tab (refer to Figure 17.5). You can select which drive to check and then start the defragmenting process (see Figure 17.6).

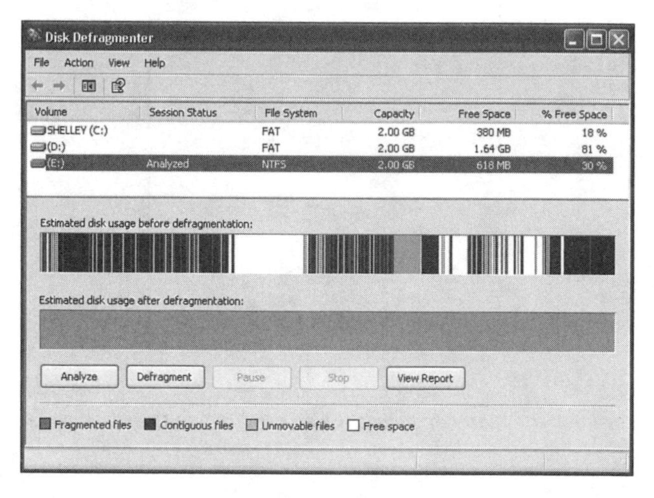


**FIGURE 17.6**
*Use Disk Defragmenter to defragment a drive to improve its performance.*

**TIP**

**Do an Analysis First** Before you defragment, analyze the disk first by clicking the **Analyze** button. Analyze provides a recommendation. Becuase defragmenting takes a long time, don't do it unless it is recommended.

Disk Defragmenter may take a while to defragment your disk, depending on the size of the disk, the number and size of files on the volume, the extent of fragmentation in the disk, and available system resources. Disk Defragmenter's progress is indicated by the progress bar in the Disk Defragmenter window. When the process completes, Disk Defragmenter displays the results. Click **View Report**. The Defragmentation Report dialog box displays detailed information about the disk that was defragmented. Click the **Close** button to close the report, and then the Defragmenter window.

## Using System Restore

If you add new programs or hardware, you might find that your system does not work properly. Trying to troubleshoot a problem such as this can be difficult. To help, Windows XP includes System Restore, which you can use to go back to a previous setup that did work. Using System Restore enables you to preserve recent work, such as saved documents, e-mail messages, history lists, or favorites lists.

Instead of relying on you to create backups, System Restore monitors changes to your system, and creates *restore points* each day by default. There are several types of restore points:

- *Initial system checkpoint* is created the first time you start your computer after Windows XP is installed (don't select this restore point unless you want to wipe your computer clean of everything you've done on it since installing XP).
- *System checkpoints* are created by Windows every 24 hours, and every 10 hours your computer is turned on.
- *Program name installation restore points* are created automatically when you install a program using one of the latest installers. Select this restore point to remove installed programs and registry settings.
- *Manually created restore points* are those restore points you create yourself (see the following steps).

- *Restore operation restore points* track restoration operations themselves, enabling you to undo them.
- *Unsigned driver restore points* are created any time System Restore determines that you are installing an unsigned or uncertified driver.

Follow these steps to use System Restore:

1. Click the **Start** button, click **All Programs**, **Accessories**, **System Tools**, **System Restore**. You see the System Restore window (see Figure 17.7).

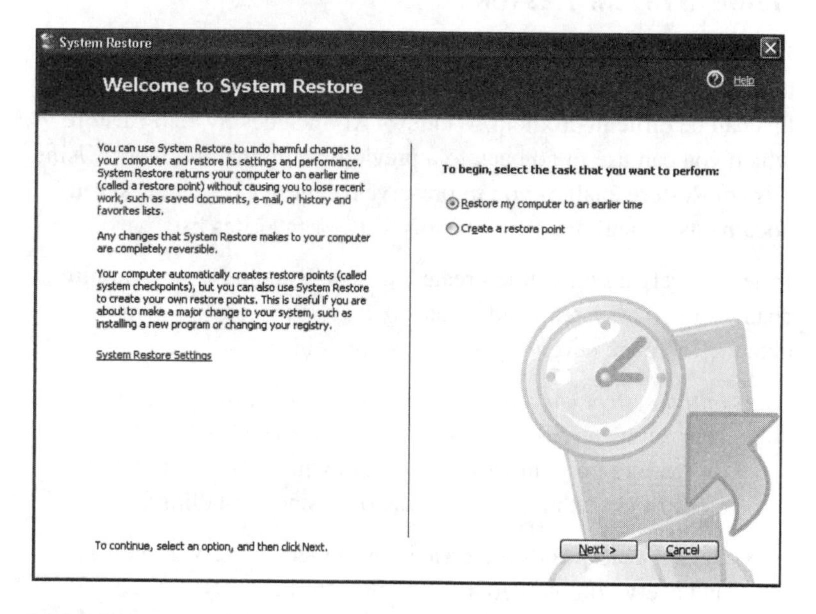


**FIGURE 17.7**

*The System Restore window gives detailed information about how to use this feature.*

**2.** Do any of the following:

To create a restore point, click **Create a restore point,** and then click **Next**. Type a restore point name and then click **Create**.

To go back to an earlier restore point, click **Restore my computer to an earlier time**. Select a date on the calendar, and then select a restore point. Follow the rest of the onscreen instructions, clicking **Next** to move from step to step. Be sure to read each explanation carefully so that you understand what will happen.

In this lesson you learned about some important maintenance as well as some troubleshooting features of Windows XP. The next lesson covers using Windows XP with multiple users and on a home network.

# Lesson 18
# Setting Up Windows for Multiple Users or Networking

*In this lesson you learn how to set up Microsoft Windows for multiple users. You also get a short overview of the home networking features of Windows XP.*

## Setting Up Windows for Multiple Users

If more than one person uses your PC, you might want to personalize certain Windows settings for each person. For example, you can customize the desktop, Start menu, Favorites folder, My Documents folder, and more. Each person can set up Windows the way he wants and then create a user account. Each time that person logs on, all those settings are used.

### Setting Up a New Account

Follow these steps to set up a new account:

1. Set up Windows the way you like it.
2. Click **Start** and then click **Control Panel**.
3. Click **User Accounts** in the Control Panel window. Any accounts you have created are listed (see Figure 18.1).

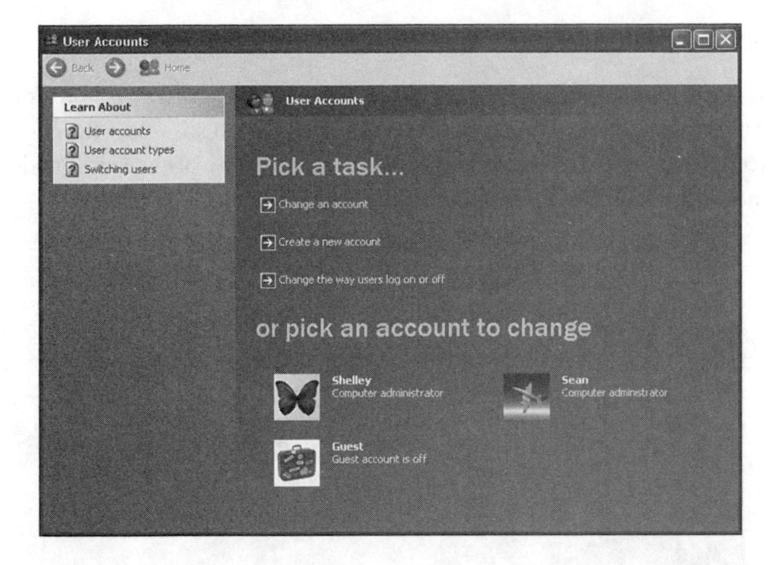


**FIGURE 18.1**
*You can use this Control Panel option to modify existing accounts and set up new accounts.*

4. Click the **Create a new account** link.
5. Type a name for the account and click the **Next** button.
6. Select what type of account you want to create: Computer administrator or Limited. When you select an account type, you see a description of what that account can and cannot do. Click the **Create Account** button. The new account is added.

**CAUTION**

**Pick One Computer Administrator** Having one person as the computer administrator is best. This person can create new accounts and modify and delete existing accounts. For all others, consider making them limited accounts so that these users cannot mess around with the other accounts.

## MODIFYING AN ACCOUNT

You can make changes to existing accounts, specifying a password for that account, changing the picture, and so on. To do so, select the account in the User Accounts window. Then use any of the commands shown in Figure 18.2 to do the following:

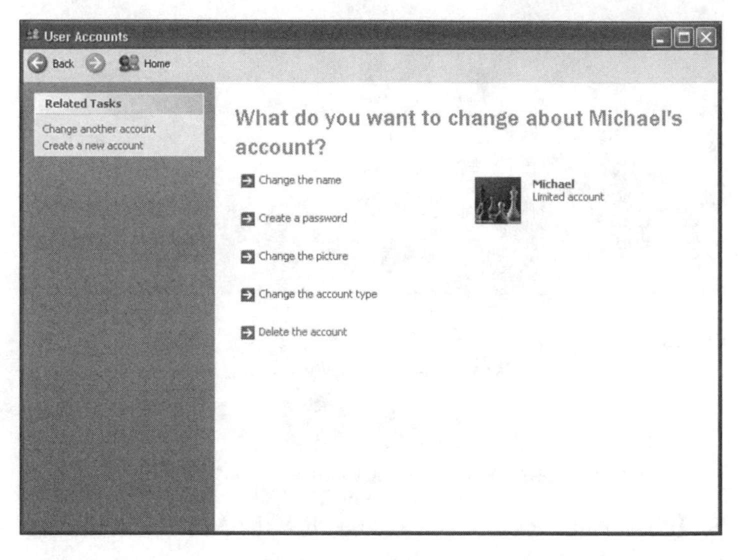


**FIGURE 18.2**
*You can make changes to existing accounts in the User Accounts window.*

- To change the name of the account, click **Change the name**, type a new name, and then click the **Change Name** button.
- To create a password for this account, click **Create a password**. Type the password you want to use and type it again to confirm. Type a hint to help you remember the password by offering you a visible clue on the Windows login screen, and then click the **Create Password** button.
- To use a different picture for the account, click **Change the picture**. Then select from one of the available pictures. You

can also click **Browse for more pictures** to select another picture (a photograph, for example) stored in another location. After you select the picture, click the **Change Picture** button.

- To change the type of account, click **Change the account type**. You can then select computer administrator or limited. When you select an option, Windows XP displays a description of that account type.
- To delete the account, click **Delete the account**. Select whether to keep or delete the account files. Then click the **Delete Account** button.

### Logging On and Off

If you have set up accounts, you see the different account names when you turn on your computer. You can click your account to log on. You can also switch from one user account to another. When you switch users, all open programs remain open. When you log off, everything is shut down. To log on or off, follow these steps:

1. Click the **Start** button and click **Log Off**.
2. When asked if you're sure you want to log off, click the **Log Off** button.
3. When prompted, select the account you want to log in under.

## Home Networking Basics

If your household contains multiple computers (one equipped with Windows XP, and at least one more equipped with XP/2000, Windows Me, or Windows 9x), you can connect them to create a home network. Doing so enables you to share an Internet connection, hardware (such as a printer, scanner, and so on), and files and folders. Networking the computers in your home also enables members of your household to play multi-computer games.

**TIP**

**Internet Access and Networks** If you have a network and want all PCs on it to have access to the Internet, you have two options. One is to pick a hosting Windows XP computer and share that Internet connection with the other PCs on the network. The other is to use a device called a ***router***, which distributes your Internet connection to all the PCs on your network without one of them having to play the role of host.

Setting up a home network involves three basic steps: planning your network, installing and configuring the appropriate network hardware on each computer on the network, and running the Windows XP Network Setup wizard. Although an in-depth discussion of the first and second steps is beyond the scope of this book, you will find ample information about it in Windows XP's Help area (click the **Networking and the Web** link in the main Help and Support page).

When planning your network, you must determine what type of network you want to build (Ethernet, HPNA or home phone line networking, or wireless), and decide which machine serves as your host computer (it should run Windows XP). In terms of installing and configuring the appropriate network hardware, note that you must equip each computer on your network with a network interface card (NIC), also called a *network adapter*. Additionally, if you want to network more than two PCs, you need a *hub* or *switch*, which is a separate box into which cables from each network card connect. Many retail home networking kits contain the cards and the hub, as well as setup instructions.

The third step, in which you run the Windows XP Network Setup wizard on each computer you want on the network, enables you to quickly and easily configure each PC for networking, making the task of setting up your home network far less difficult and intimidating than you might think.

PLAIN ENGLISH

**Hub Versus Switch** The difference between a hub and switch is that a switch is, more or less, a "smart" hub. When one computer sends a request to or shares data with another computer, a hub sends it to every computer on the network, relying on the PC the data is meant for to recognize and respond to it. A switch learns which computer is which and sends that data only to the PC for which it is intended.

The Network Setup wizard is covered in the following section, as are the tasks associated with using a home network, including accessing network files.

## Using the Network Setup Wizard

After you have installed the necessary networking hardware, you can configure each computer to use the network by working through the Network Setup Wizard. This wizard automates several procedures that were once done manually in earlier versions of Windows, including configuring your network adapters, configuring all your computers to share a single Internet connection, naming each computer, setting up file and printer sharing, installing a firewall, and more.

Follow these steps to run the Network Setup Wizard:

1. Click **Start**, **All Programs**, **Accessories**, **Communications**, **Network Setup Wizard**.
2. Click **Next** to begin setting up your home network. Be sure you've installed all network cards, modems, and cables; turned on all computers, printers, and external modems; and connected to the Internet. Then click **Next**.
3. Complete each step in the wizard, answering the questions based on your particular setup and clicking **Next** to move to the next step. You can expect to select

- How your PC connects to the Internet (see Figure 18.3)

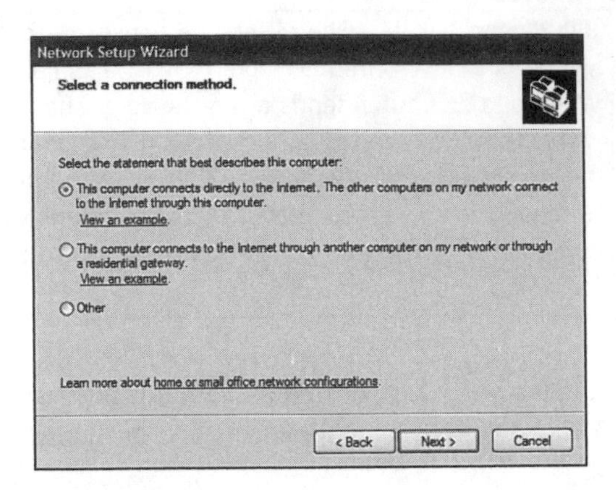


**FIGURE 18.3**
*A networked computer should either have a direct Internet connection or a connection through another PC or router. This dialog box lets you tell Windows XP which this is.*

- The type of computer you are configuring
- Enter a name and description of the computer
- Name the network you are creating
- Confirm the settings for this network
- Then configure all other computers hooked up to the network

When the setup is complete, you see the Finish button. You then need to restart to finish the setup and start the configuration setup for all other connected computers.

## SHARING FILES

By default, certain folders are made available to all computers on your network. To make other folders on a computer available to other machines on your network, you must enable file sharing for those folders. (You need to perform this task on all networked computers that contain folders that you want to make available over the network.)

To share files, follow these steps:

1. Right-click the folder you want to share on your network and click the **Sharing and Security** command. The folder's Properties dialog box opens, with the Sharing tab displayed.
2. Check the **Share this folder on the network** check box (see Figure 18.4).

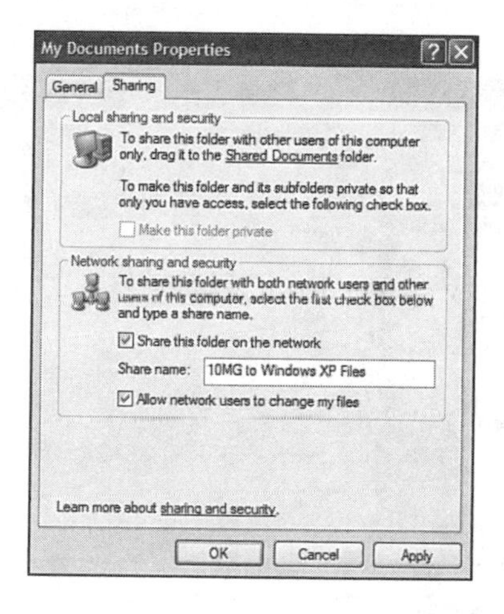


**FIGURE 18.4**
*Use the Sharing tab to enable folder sharing for the selected folder.*

3. If you want users on other machines to be able to change the contents of this folder, check the **Allow network users to change my files** check box. Then click the **OK** button.

**TIP**

**Sharing Drives and Devices** In addition to sharing folders and files, you can share drives and devices, such as printers, scanners, and so on. Follow the same steps, but instead of right-clicking a folder, right-click the drive or device instead.

You can browse shared files on the network through My Network Places. It works just like My Computer, except that it shows you files on other network computers instead of the ones on your system.

To view these files, follow these steps:

1. Click the **Start** button, and then click **My Network Places**. The My Network Places window is displayed, listing all shared folders on the network.
2. Double-click a folder icon to open that folder (see Figure 18.5).

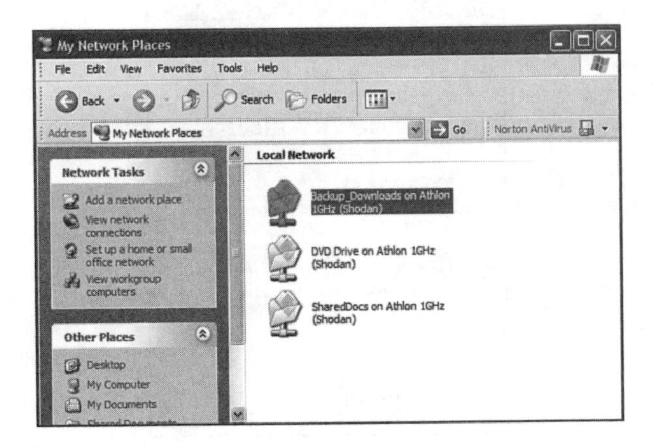


**FIGURE 18.5**
*When you open My Network Places, you see all shared folders.*

## SHARING INTERNET CONNECTIONS AND PRINTER

Some versions of AOL do not enable you to share a single Internet connection among multiple machines (contact AOL for more information). Likewise, other ISPs may charge you extra to use a single Internet connection for multiple computers.

A network printer works the same as a local printer in all your applications. Simply select **Network the printer** from the Print dialog box in whatever program you are printing from. For more information about printing, refer to Lesson 8, "Printing."

## Network Security

If your home network is connected to the Internet, you suffer an increased risk of hackers obtaining access to the computers on that network. One way to obstruct unauthorized users is to erect a *firewall*. Windows XP ships complete with a firewall that is installed automatically when you run the Network Setup Wizard on a machine with a direct connection to the Internet. For more information on Internet security, see Lesson 10, "Browsing the Internet."

TIP

**More Coverage** This lesson barely touches on all the details of networking, but you at least get the idea of what you can do. For more detailed information, consider referencing a book like ***Special Edition Using Windows XP Home Edition***, also a Que publication (ISBN#0-7897-2627-0).

This lesson covered how to set up a single computer for multiple users as well as several computers in a home network. The next lesson shows you how to set up new hardware and update hardware drivers.

# Lesson 19 Setting Up New Hardware

*In this lesson you learn how to set up new hardware as well as update hardware drivers.*

## Setting Up New Hardware

As you use your computer, you may find that you want to add new components to your system. You can purchase a digital camera or scanner (see Lesson 12, "Working with Pictures"). You can also add a DVD drive or a CD-RW drive (a recordable/rewritable drive). You might be into music (covered in Lesson 13, "Playing Music") and want to explore many of the digital music add-ons, such as MP3 or other portable music devices.

In any case, setting up new hardware can be fairly straightforward. In the best case scenario, you simply attach or install the new device and Windows XP sets it up automatically. If that doesn't happen, you can always install the device manually. Both methods are covered in this section.

### Setting Up New Hardware Automatically

To set up hardware automatically, simply follow the installation instructions for your particular device. For some add-on components, you simply connect the device to an available port. For example, most scanners plug into a USB port, while many digital video camcorders connect to your PC via a Firewire port.

**PLAIN ENGLISH**

**USB and Firewire** USB, short for universal serial bus, is a type of port found on most computers. You can connect devices to these ports by plugging in the USB cable to the USB port on your computer.

Firewire, also called IEEE 1394b, is a high-speed technology for connecting peripherals that transfers large volumes of data, like external hard disk drives or digital video camcorders. Most PCs do not come with these ports built in; rather, you must install a Firewire add-in card.

For other hardware, you may have to turn off your computer and remove the system case. For example, to install network or internal modem cards, you have to turn off the power, remove the case, and then plug the cards into slots inside of the system unit.

In either case, if Windows XP recognizes the new hardware, it automatically starts the Add Hardware Wizard and queries the device for setup information. It then installs the appropriate driver file and alerts you that the device has been found and installed. You should see alert messages in the system tray as this process is completed. You can then use your device.

**PLAIN ENGLISH**

**Driver** A driver is a special type of file that tells Windows XP the details about a particular hardware device. Windows comes with many drivers for lots of add-on components. The add-on component also usually comes with a disk that contains a driver for using the component. If Windows needs this driver, it prompts you for it during the install process.

## SETTING UP NEW HARDWARE MANUALLY

If the Add Hardware Wizard does not start and find your new hardware device automatically, you can run the wizard manually. Have Windows search for and install the new device or select the device manufacturer and product from a list. Follow these steps:

1. Open the Start menu, right-click the **My Computer** icon and select **Properties**. In the System Properties dialog box, click the **Hardware** tab (see Figure 19.1). Then click the **Add Hardware Wizard** button.

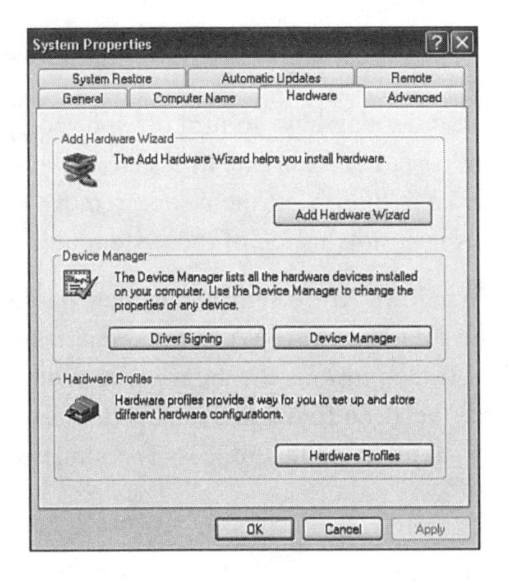


**FIGURE 19.1**
*You can access the Hardware Wizard from either the System Properties dialog box (shown here) or from the Control Panel.*

Or

Click **Start**, and then **Control Panel**. Click **Printers and Other Hardware**. In the See Also area of the task pane, click **Add Hardware**.

Both display the first step of the Add Hardware Wizard.

**TIP**

**Use Hardware Disk** The opening screen of the Add Hardware Wizard recommends using the disk that came with the hardware to install and set up the device. You can also use this method. To do so, follow the specific instructions for your particular hardware component.

2. Click **Next** to move past the welcome screen. You are asked whether the device is already connected (see Figure 19.2).

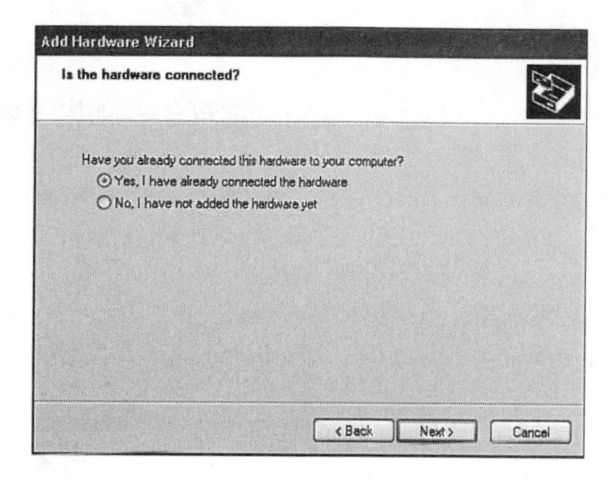


**FIGURE 19.2**
*Windows XP first wants to know whether the device is connected.*

3. If your device is an external USB or Firewire device, make sure it is connected and then click **Yes, I have already connected the hardware**. If your device is installed internally or connected to your computer's parallel or other port, you should first power off your PC before installing or connecting it. Click **Next** to move to the next step. You see a list of all the devices already installed. (You can use this list to troubleshoot any device problems. See "Troubleshooting Hardware Problems" later in this lesson.) Figure 19.3 shows this step.

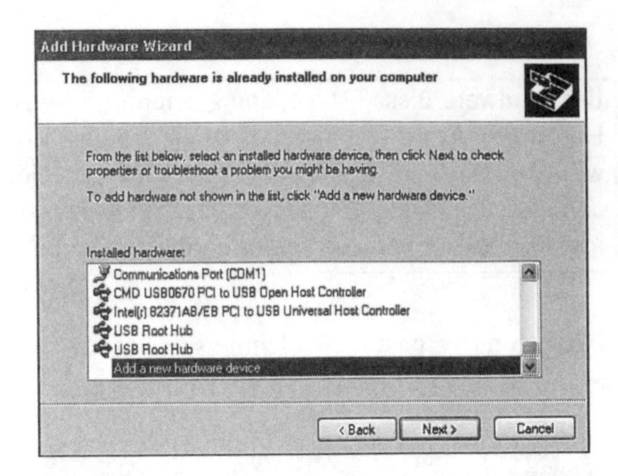


**FIGURE 19.3**
*To add new hardware, select the last option in the list of hardware devices.*

4. Select **Add a new hardware device** and click **Next**. You have the choice of letting Windows XP search for the new device and set it up automatically or to set up the device manually (see Figure 19.4). Try searching first. To use the manual method, select this option and skip to step 6.

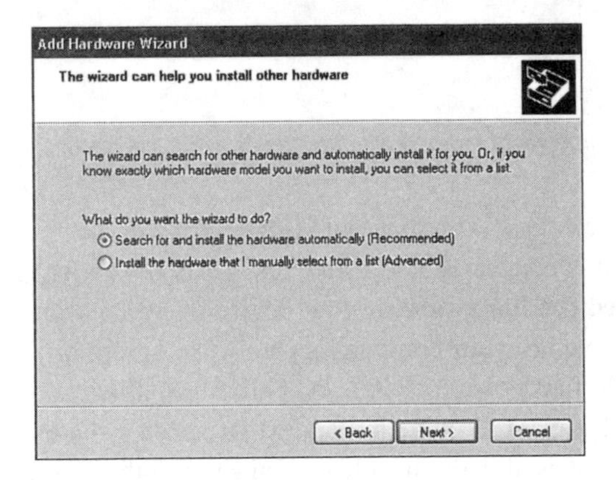


**FIGURE 19.4**
*Windows provides two methods for finding and installing the hardware: automatic and manual.*

5. Select the automatic (recommended) option and click **Next**. Windows XP searches for new devices. If the device is found, Windows XP then installs the new device. Follow the remaining prompts to complete setup.

6. If the hardware device is not found, click **Next**. You see a list of command hardware categories. You also see this same list if you selected to set up the hardware manually in step 4. Figure 19.5 shows the list.

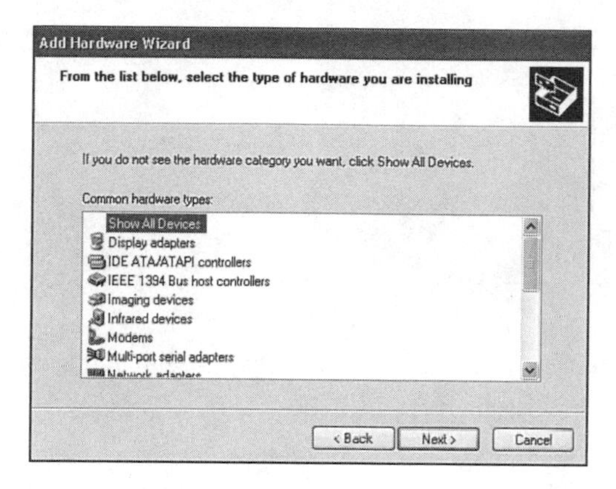


**FIGURE 19.5**
*You can select the type of hardware from a list of common devices.*

7. Select your device type and click **Next**. You are prompted to select the manufacturer and model of the device you are installing (see Figure 19.6).

**CAUTION**

**Device not listed?** If your device type is not listed, click **Show All Devices**, and then click **Next**.

8. Scroll through the list of manufacturers until you see the manufacturer of your device. Then click it. You then see

available models from this manufacturer in the Model list. Click the model and click **Next**. Follow the onscreen instructions for completing the installation of your device. You can then use your new hardware device.

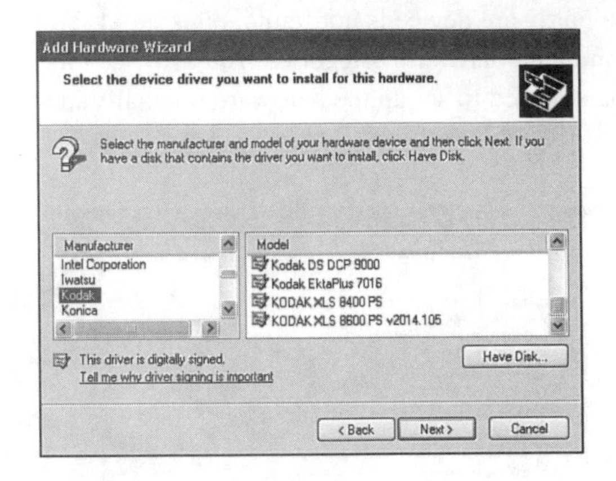


**FIGURE 19.6**
*Select the manufacturer and then model of the device from this list.*

**TIP**

**Use Disk** If your device manufacturer or type is not listed in this dialog box, but you do have a drive disk that came with your device, click the **Have Disk** button and follow the onscreen instructions. If you don't have an up-to-date driver disk with your device, try looking for a downloadable version from the manufacturer's Web site.

## UPDATING AND TROUBLESHOOTING DEVICES

You can view a list of installed devices on your computer. You might do this to see information about the device—for example, whether it is enabled or not. You might do this if you need to update a driver for the device or to get troubleshooting help on a particular device.

To start, display the Device Manager by following these steps:

1. Click the **Start** button, right-click the **My Computer** icon and then select **Properties** to display the System Properties dialog box. Then click the **Hardware** tab (refer to Figure 19.1).

2. Click the **Device Manager** button. You see the Device Manager listing the categories of hardware devices. Each category has a plus sign next to it. You can click this plus sign to expand the list and see the device(s) installed for each category. Figure 19.7 shows the Modems category expanded.

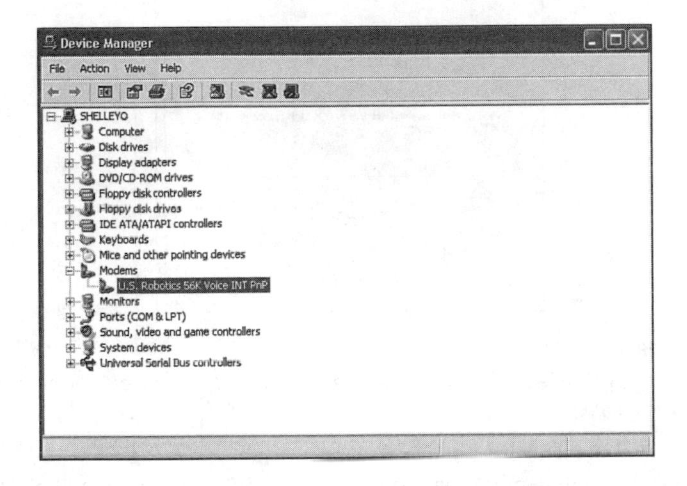


**FIGURE 19.7**
*You can expand and collapse the hardware device list to see device(s) in each category.*

3. To make changes or view information about a particular device, click it in the list. You can then use the menus in the Device Manager window to make changes. As another alternative, you can right-click the device to display the shortcut menu.

## VIEWING DEVICE PROPERTIES

To display information about a device, right-click the device and select **Properties** or click the device, and then click the **Action**, **Properties** command. In either case, you see the Properties dialog box for the selected device. Figure 19.8 shows the properties dialog box for a modem.

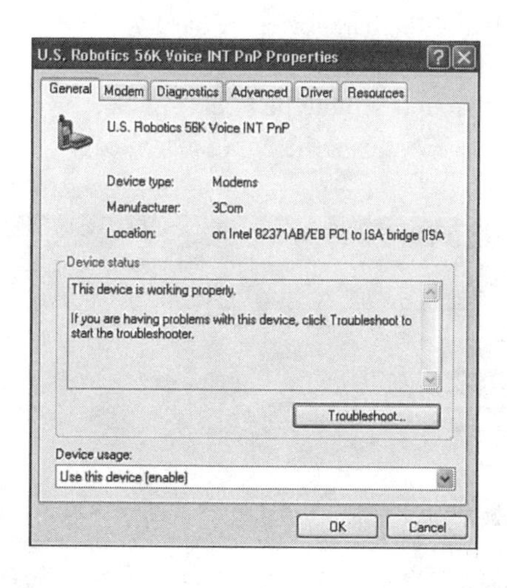


**FIGURE 19.8**

*You can view detailed information about an installed device by displaying its properties dialog box.*

The tabs vary depending on the selected device, but you can click each tab to view information. For modems, for example, the General tab lists the type of device, manufacturer, and location (how it is connected). You also see the status of the device. You can click the **Modem** tab to set speaker volume, maximum port speed, and dial control. (Again, remember that these tabs and options vary depending on what you have selected.) Use the Advanced tab to type in special modem commands or set advanced settings for the port. Use the Driver tab to view driver information (see the section "Updating Device Drivers."). The Resources tab lists technical information such as the memory and IRQ settings (you should not need to modify these settings). Use the Diagnostics tab to diagnose problems with the modem.

## Troubleshooting Device Problems

If you are having problems with a particular hardware device, you can use one of Windows XP troubleshooters to display common problems as well as solutions. You can access this troubleshooter from the Device Manager.

TIP

**Troubleshoot from the Add Hardware Wizard** You can also troubleshoot a device using the Add Hardware Wizard. When the list of installed devices is displayed, select the device with problems, and then follow the onscreen prompts for displaying help.

Follow these steps:

1. Right-click the device and select **Properties**. Then click the **Troubleshoot** button on the properties dialog box (refer to Figure 19.8). Doing so launches the Windows XP help system and displays troubleshooting information (see Figure 19.9).
2. Select your problem from the list and then click **Next**. Windows XP displays queries you to try to determine the problem. Answer the questions, clicking **Next** to go to the next step. When Windows identifies the problem, it recommends some ways to solve that problem. Try any recommended fixes. You may have to step through several pages of questions and help suggestions until the problem is fixed.

   For example, if your problem with your modem is getting connected to the Internet, Windows XP asks whether the modem makes any sounds. If you select **No**, Windows XP suggests that you verify the modem is connected properly. If you do so, you can then select from several options in the troubleshooter (see Figure 19.10). Selecting **Yes** solves the problem. You can skip this recommended solution or you can click **No** to display other possible solutions.

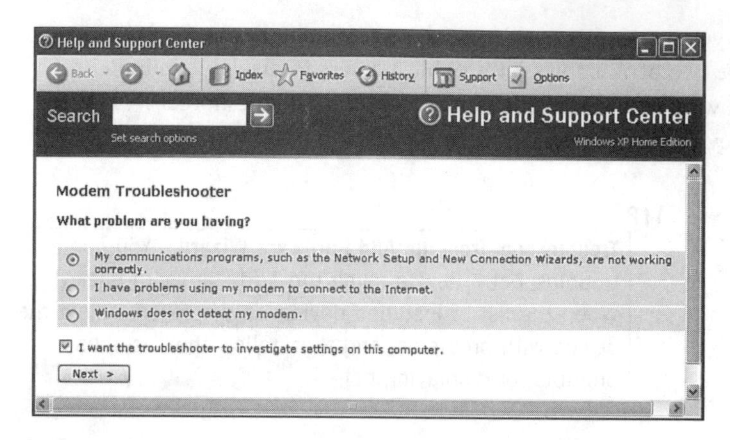


**FIGURE 19.9**
*Use the troubleshooter to select your problem, and then get possible solutions for that problem.*

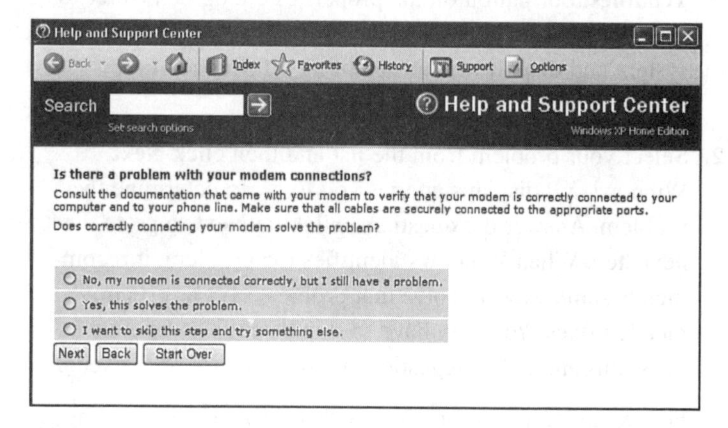


**FIGURE 19.10**
*If the first solution doesn't work, you can have Windows display other possible solutions.*

**Get Help** You can also access the troubleshooting information by using the Help command. See Lesson 17, "Maintaining Your PC."

If the Windows XP troubleshooters are unable to identify your hardware problem, you are told to contact technical support. While Microsoft technical support can probably help you with your problem, your best bet is to contact the support department for the manufacturer of your device (this information should be available in the documentation or at the manufacturer's Web site).

## Updating Device Drivers

Sometimes if a device is not working properly, you may need to remove, and then reinstall it. For example, if a device works sporadically, you may want to remove it from the Windows XP setup, and then try reinstalling it. As another option, you may want ask Windows XP to scan the particular hardware for changes. If the device is causing so much havoc but you don't have time to fix it or you need to wait to get an updated hardware driver, you may want to disable it (turn it off so that the driver is still installed, but the device is not available).

You can do any of these things by displaying the Device Manager. Then right-click the device and select the appropriate command. You can select **Disable**, **Uninstall**, or Scan for hardware changes. For each command, you are prompted to confirm your actions. For example, if you uninstall a device, you are prompted to confirm the removal.

Another fix is to update the device driver. As mentioned previously in this lesson, the device driver is a file that tells Windows XP the technical details about the particular device. Windows XP comes with many device drivers. The hardware component you add also usually has a disk with its particular device drivers. These are updated periodically if the device has problems (called *bugs*) or if Windows is updated.

Updating drivers when a new version of Windows, such as Windows XP, is released is common. Microsoft tests and provides many drivers, but it cannot test all possible hardware add-ons. Therefore, the manufacturer of a device often releases new drivers to work with the new version of Windows.

To update your driver, follow these steps:

1. Display the Device Manager.
2. Right-click the device and select **Update Driver**. When you select Update Driver, Windows XP starts the Hardware Update Wizard (see Figure 19.11).

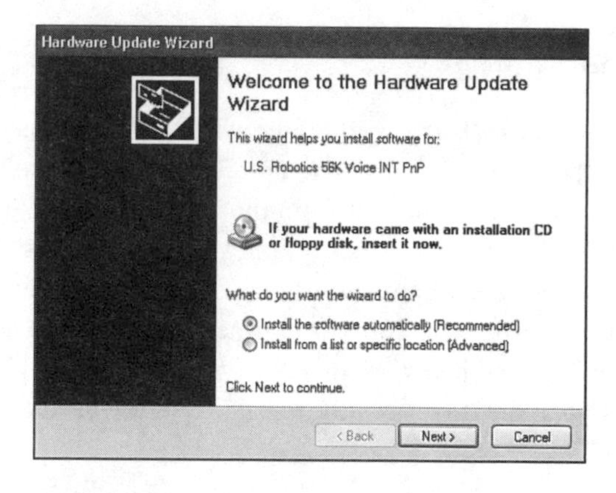


**FIGURE 19.11**
*Use the Hardware Update Wizard to update your driver.*

**TIP**

**Use Drivers Tab** You can also display the Properties dialog box for the device, click the **Driver** tab, and use the buttons on that tab to update drivers.

3. Follow the steps in the wizard, making your selections and clicking **Next** to move from step to step.

**Hardware Update Wizard** The Hardware Update Wizard only checks for Windows-certified drivers. It is possible the manufacturer of your device has released updated drivers that Microsoft has not yet had time to certify. In this case, you should visit the hardware manufacturer's Web site to download their driver (be sure it is designed for Windows XP first). Instructions for installing it properly should also be found on their Web site.

This lesson covered how to set up new hardware. The next lesson covers using special options for users with disabilities. Windows XP includes several Accessibility Accessories programs as well as Control Panel features.

# LESSON 20
# Using Accessibility Features

*In this lesson you learn how to use the Accessibility Accessories programs and Control Panel options to set up Windows for users with special needs.*

## USING ACCESSIBILITY PROGRAMS

Windows XP offers programs that make it easier for those with disabilities to use the operating system. Magnifier magnifies the contents of your screen, Narrator reads the contents of your screen aloud, and On-Screen keyboard enables users who have limited mobility to type onscreen using a pointing device.

TIP

**Manage Accessibility Programs** You can manage the three accessibility programs using Utility Manager. You can also use the Accessibility Wizard to set up and turn on any of the programs. To use these programs, select them from the Accessibility menu.

To start any of these accessory programs, follow these steps:

1. Click the **Start** button, select **All Programs**, choose **Accessories**, and then click **Accessibility**.
2. Click any of the programs: **Magnifier**, **Narrator**, or **On-Screen keyboard**. The particular program is started.

**CAUTION**

**Informational Dialog Boxes** When you start each program, you may notice the appearance of a dialog box that provides information about the program you opened. Simply read over the contents of the dialog box, and click the **OK** button to close it.

**TIP**

**Minimize Program** To keep the program open, but remove the program's dialog box from view, click the **Minimize** button in the top-right corner of the dialog box.

## Using Magnifier

Magnifier magnifies part of your screen so that you can better see the screen. The top part of the screen shows the location of the mouse pointer. The rest of the screen shows the "regular" view of the window. In Figure 20.1, for example, you see the Display Properties dialog box open. The magnification area shows the location of the mouse pointer. You can use this tool to better see and select options.

To fine-tune this program, you can use the Magnifier Settings dialog box, shown in Figure 20.2. This dialog box appears when you start the program. Do any of the following:

- To change the magnification level, display the drop-down list and select a different level. The higher the level, the bigger the current pointer location appears.
- By default, Magnifier automatically follows the mouse cursor, keyboard focus, and text editing. To turn off any tracking options, uncheck them.
- By default, the Magnifier Settings dialog box is displayed. You can choose to start the program minimized. You can also invert the colors. To do so, check any of these options in the Presentation area of the dialog box.

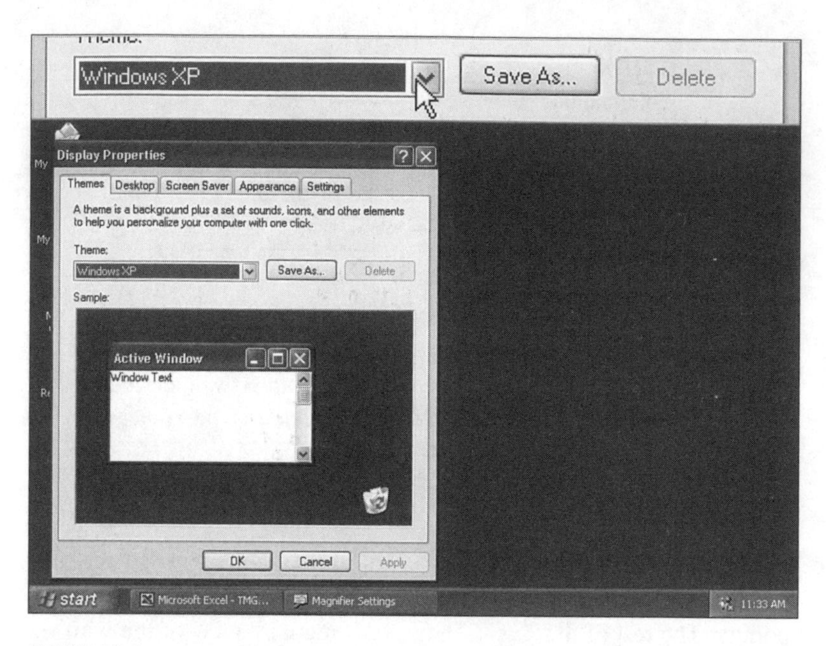


**FIGURE 20.1**
*You can magnify the current location of the mouse pointer so that you can better see and select options.*

To exit Magnifier, click the **Exit** button in the Magnifier Settings dialog box.

## USING NARRATOR

When you start Narrator, you see the opening screen. Click **OK**. You see the Narrator dialog box, shown in Figure 20.3, and the Narrator reads by default events on screen and typed characters.

You can also have Narrator move the mouse pointer to the active item. As another option, you can start the program minimized. Check any of the desired options in the Narrator dialog box.

You can select a voice you want to use for Narrator, as well as the speed, volume, and pitch of that voice. To do so, click the **Voice** button in the Narrator dialog box. A Voice Settings dialog box opens; select your settings, and then click the **OK** button.

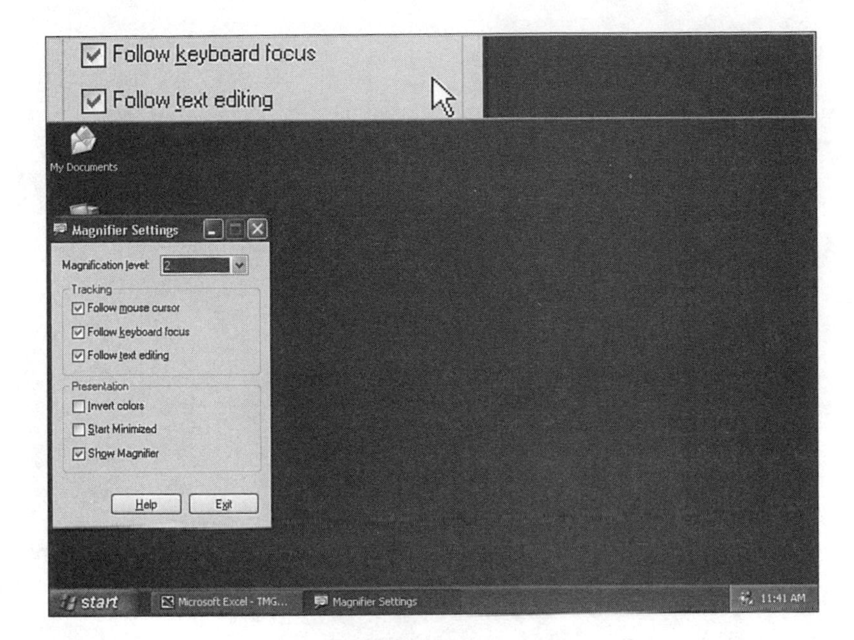


**FIGURE 20.2**
*Use the Magnifier Settings dialog box to make changes to how this program works.*

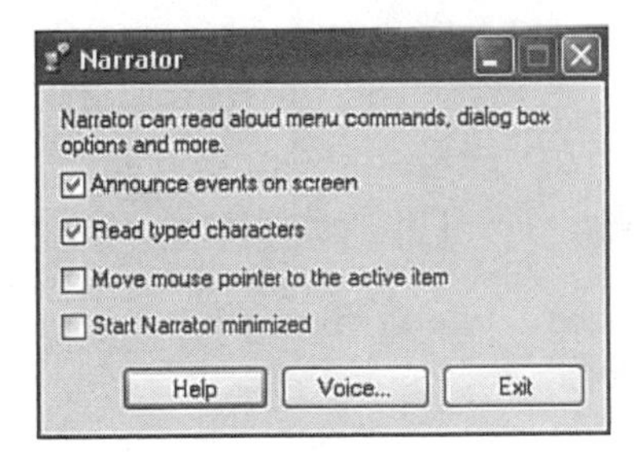


**FIGURE 20.3**
*Use Narrator to have the program announce events including reading dialog box options as well as typed characters.*

To exit the program, click the **Exit** button. Then click **Yes** to confirm you want to exit.

### USING ON-SCREEN KEYBOARD

When you start On-Screen Keyboard, you see the welcome screen which describes its use. Click **OK** to close the dialog box. You can then use the On-Screen Keyboard, shown in Figure 20.4, to type.

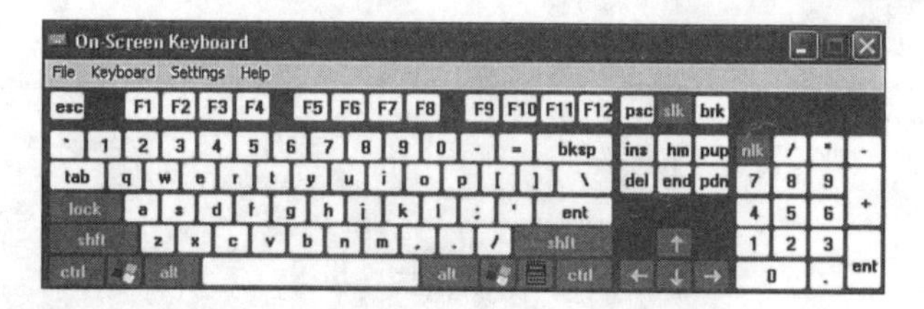

**FIGURE 20.4**
*You can use On-Screen Keyboard to type using your mouse.*

You can type by clicking the onscreen keys with your mouse pointer. If you prefer a different method, you can click **Settings**, **Typing Mode** to select another method: **Hover** or **Scanning**. In hovering mode, you use a mouse or joystick to hover the pointer over a key; the selected character is then typed. In scanning mode, On-Screen Keyboard scans the keyboard, highlighting letters; you press a hotkey or use a switch-input device whenever On-Screen Keyboard highlights the character you want to type.

## USING ACCESSIBILITY CONTROL PANEL OPTIONS

In addition to the accessory programs, you can also use one of several Control Panel options. To view and select these options, follow these steps:

1. Click **Start**, **Control Panel**.
2. In the Control Panel Window, click **Accessibility Options**.

3. In the Accessibility Options window, click **Accessibility Options** again. You see the Accessibility Options dialog box (see Figure 20.5).

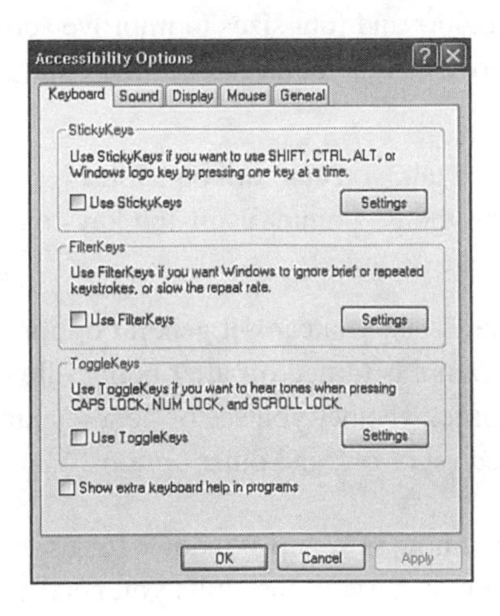


**FIGURE 20.5**
*Select the tab, and then turn on the options you want to use.*

4. By default, the Keyboard tab is displayed. Click any of the tabs and turn on any additional options by checking the appropriate check box.

5. Click **OK**.

You can select the following options:

- On the Keyboard tab, you can turn on StickyKeys (allows you to press one key at a time instead of simultaneous keystrokes), FilterKeys (ignores brief or repeated keystrokes), or ToggleKeys (plays tones when you press **Caps Lock**, **Num Lock**, or **Scroll Lock**).
- On the Sound tab, you can turn on the SoundSentry (displays visual warnings in conjunction with playing system sounds)

or ShowSounds (instructs programs to display captions for sounds).

- On the Display tab, you can turn on High Contrast (uses alternative colors and font sizes to improve screen contrast). You can also select the blink rate for the cursor as well as its width.
- On the Mouse tab, you can turn on MouseKeys if you want to control the mouse pointer using the keys on the numeric keypad.
- On the General tab, you can set general options such as whether a feature is turned off after being idle for a set amount of time, whether you see or hear a sound when a feature is turned on or off, and other options.

This lesson covered how to set up Windows for users with special needs. You should now have all the skills you need to use Windows XP for fun, successful, and stress-free computing. Enjoy!

# INDEX

## A

## B

## C

## D

## E



## F

## G-H

## I-J



## K-L

## M



## N



## O

## P-Q

## R



## S

## T



## U

## V



## W-Z